COGAT™
TEST PREP
GRADE 6

COGAT® TEST PREP GRADE 6
Level 12

Gateway Gifted Resources™
www.GatewayGifted.com

PLEASE LEAVE
US A REVIEW!

Thank you for selecting this book. We are a family-owned publishing company - a consortium of educators, test designers, book designers, parents, and kid-testers.

We would be thrilled if you left us a quick review on the website where you purchased this book!

The Gateway Gifted Resources™ Team
www.GatewayGifted.com

TABLE OF CONTENTS

ABOUT THIS BOOK: This book helps prepare kids for the COGAT® Level 12, a test given to sixth graders. Not only will this publication help prepare children for the COGAT®, these logic-based exercises may also be used for other gifted test preparation and as critical thinking exercises. This book has five parts.

1. Introduction (p.4-9): About this book & the COGAT®, Test Taking Tips, and Question Examples

2. Practice Test 1 (Workbook Format): These pages are designed similarly to content tested in the COGAT®'s nine test question types. Unless you already have experience with COGAT® prep materials, you should complete Practice Test 1 (Workbook Format) together with no time limit. **Before doing this section, read the Question Examples & Explanations (p.5).**

3. Practice Test 2: Practice Test 2 helps kids develop critical thinking and test-taking skills. It provides an introduction in a relaxed manner (parents provide guidance if needed) and an opportunity for kids to focus on a group of questions for a longer time period. This part is also a way for you to identify points of strength/ challenges in COGAT® question types. Practice Test 2 is divided into three sections to mirror the three COGAT® batteries: Verbal, Quantitative, and Non-Verbal.

4. Answer Keys: These pages contain the Practice Test answers as well as brief answer explanations.

ABOUT THE COGAT® LEVEL 12: The COGAT® (Cognitive Abilities Test®) test is divided into 3 "batteries."

- *Verbal Battery; total time: around 45 minutes*

Question Types (15 minutes each, approximately): Verbal Analogies, Verbal Classification, Sentence Completion

- *Non-Verbal Battery; total time: around 45 minutes*

Question Types (15 minutes each, approximately): Figure Analogies, Figure Classification, Paper Folding

- *Quantitative Battery; total time: around 45 minutes*

Question Types (15 minutes each, approximately): Number Series, Number Puzzles, Number Analogies

The test has 176 questions total. The test is administered in different testing sessions. Kids are not expected to finish 176 questions in one session.

ABOUT COGAT® TESTING PROCEDURES: These vary by school. Tests may be given individually or in a group. These tests may be used as the single factor for admission to gifted programs, or they may be used in combination with IQ tests or as part of a student "portfolio." They are used by some schools together with tests like Iowa Assessments™. Check with your testing site to determine its specific testing procedures.

QUESTION NOTE: Because each person has different cognitive abilities, the questions in this book are at varied skill levels. The exercises may or may not require a great deal of parental guidance to complete, depending on your kid's abilities, prior test prep experience, or prior testing experience. Most sections of the Workbook begin with a relatively easy question. We suggest always completing at least the first question together, ensuring there's not any confusion about what the question asks or with the directions.

SCORING NOTE: Check with your school/program for its scoring procedure and admissions requirements. Here is a general summary of the COGAT® scoring process. First, your child's raw score is established. This is the number of questions correctly answered. Points are not deducted for questions answered incorrectly. Next, this score is compared to other test-takers of his/her same age group (and, for the COGAT®, the same grade level) using various indices to then calculate your child's stanine (a score from one to nine) and percentile rank. If your child achieved the percentile rank of 98%, then (s)he scored as well as or better than 98% of test-takers. In general, gifted programs accept scores of *at least* 98% or *higher*. Please note that a percentile rank "score" cannot be obtained from our practice material. This material has not been given to a large enough sample of test-takers to develop any kind of base score necessary for percentile rank calculations.

QUESTION EXAMPLES & EXPLANATIONS   This section introduces the nine COGAT® question types with simple examples/explanations. Questions in Practice Test 1 & 2 will be more challenging than those below.

VERBAL BATTERY

1. VERBAL ANALOGIES   Directions: Look at the first set of words. Try to figure out how they belong together. Next, look at the second set of words. The answer is missing. Figure out which answer choice would make the second set go together in the same way that the first set goes together.

toe > foot : petal > ?   stem   bee   leg   flower   colorful

Explanation: Here are some strategies to help select the correct answer:
• Try to come up with a "rule" describing how the first set goes together. Take this rule, apply it to the first word in the second set. Determine which answer choice makes the second set follow the same "rule." If more than one choice works, you need a more specific rule. Here, a "rule" for the first set is that "the first word (toe) is part of the second word (foot)." In the next set, using this rule, "flower" is the answer. A petal is part of a flower.
• Another strategy is to come up with a sentence describing how the first set of words go together. A sentence would be: A toe is part of a foot. Then, take this sentence and apply it to the word in the second set: A petal is part of a ?. Figure out which answer choice would best complete the sentence. (It would be "flower.")
• Ensure you do not choose a word simply because it *has to do with* the first set. For example, choice A ("stem") *has to do with* a petal, but does not follow the rule.

The simple examples will introduce you to analogical thinking. Read the "Question" then "Answer Choices". Which choice goes best? (The answer is underlined.)

Analogy Logic	Question	Answer Choices (Answer is Underlined)			
• Antonyms	On *is to* Off -as- Hot *is to* ?	Warm	Sun	<u>Cold</u>	Oven
• Synonyms	Big *is to* Large -as- Horrible *is to* ?	Tired	Stale	Sour	<u>Awful</u>
• Whole: Part	Tree *is to* Branch -as- House *is to* ?	Street	Apartment	<u>Room</u>	Home
• Degree	Good *is to* Excellent -as- Tired *is to* ?	Boring	<u>Exhausted</u>	Drowsy	Slow
• Object: Location	Sun *is to* Sky -as- Swing *is to* ?	<u>Playground</u>	Monkey Bars	Sidewalk	Grass
• Same Animal Class	Turkey *is to* Parrot -as- Ant *is to* ?	Worm	<u>Beetle</u>	Duck	Spider
• Object: Creator	Painting *is to* Artist -as- Furniture *is to* ?	<u>Carpenter</u>	Tool	Chair	Potter
• Object: Container	Ice Cube *is to* Ice Tray -as- Flower *is to* ?	Petal	<u>Vase</u>	Smell	Florist
• Tool: Worker	Paintbrush *is to* Artist -as- Microscope *is to* ?	Telescope	<u>Scientist</u>	Lab	Fireman
• Object: 3D Shape	Ball *is to* Sphere -as- Dice *is to* ?	Line	Square	Cone	<u>Cube</u>
• Object: Location Used	Jet *is to* Sky -as- Canoe *is to* ?	Boat	Paddle	<u>Water</u>	Sail
• Object: Location Used	Chalk *is to* Chalkboard -as- Paintbrush *is to* ?	Artist	<u>Easel</u>	Paint	Eraser

2. VERBAL CLASSIFICATION   Directions: Look at the three words on the top row. Figure out how the words are alike. Next, look at the words in the answer choices. Which word goes best with the three words in the top row?

cake   bread   muffin

A. bakery   B. sherbet   C. cookie   D. syrup   E. sugar

Explanation: Come up with a "rule" describing how they're alike. Then, see which answer choice follows the rule. If more than one choice does, you need a more specific rule.
• At first, test-takers may say the rule for the top words is that "they are all a kind of food." However, more than one answer choice would fit this rule. A more specific rule is needed. A more specific rule would be that "the foods are baked foods." Therefore, the best answer is "cookie."
• Ensure you do not choose a word simply because it has to do with the top three. For example, choice A (bakery) has to do with the three, as all three could be found at a bakery. However, "bakery" is not a baked food.
Another simple example:

fall   spring   summer

A. warm   B. season   C. month   D. winter   E. weather

This example demonstrates a common mistake. Note answer choice "B", season. Here, the question logic (or, rule) is "seasons." A test-taker, having the rule "seasons" in their mind, may mistakenly choose "season." However, the answer is "winter," because "winter," like the top three words, is an *example* of a season.

3. SENTENCE COMPLETION **Directions:** First, read the sentence. There is a missing word. Which answer choice goes best in the sentence?

If you aren't _____ with the vase, it will break.
A. careless   B. careful   C. clear   D. risky   E. sloppy

Explanation: Here, you must use the information in the sentence and make inferences (i.e., make a best guess based on the information) and select the best answer choice to fill in the blank. Be sure to:
• pay attention to each word in the sentence and to each answer choice
• after making a choice, re-read the complete sentence to ensure the choice makes the *most* sense compared to the other choices (the answer is B)

NON-VERBAL BATTERY

4. FIGURE ANALOGIES **Directions:** Look at the top set of pictures. They go together in some way. Look at the bottom set. The answer is missing. Figure out which answer choice would make the bottom set go together in the same way that the top set goes together.

Explanation: Come up with a "rule" describing how the top set is related. This "rule" shows how the figures in the left box "change" into the figures in the right box. On the left are 2 pentagons. On the right are 3 pentagons. The rule/change is that one more of the same kind of shape is added. On the bottom are 2 rectangles. The first choice is incorrect, it shows 3 pentagons (not the same shape). The second choice is incorrect (it only shows 2 rectangles). The third choice is incorrect - it has 2 pentagons. The last choice correct. It has one more of the same shapes from the left box.

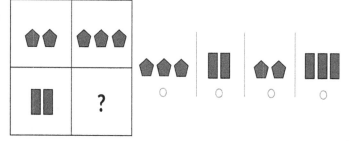

is

Here's another simple example:

In the top left box, we see 1 star. In the top right box, we also see a star, but it has gotten bigger. Let's come up with a rule to describe how the picture has changed from left to right. From left to right, the shape gets bigger. The last choice follows the rule. It is the same shape as the bottom box, but it is bigger.

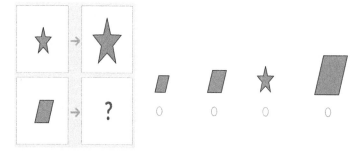

Here's another example:
In the top left box, we see a heart. In the top right box, the heart rotates 180 degrees and a vertical line is added in the center. Look at the bottom left box and the answer choices. Which answer choice follows this rule? It's C.

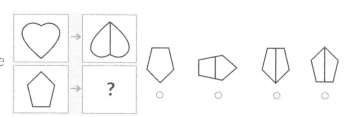

This last one is more challenging. In the top left box we see a larger square with vertical, curvy lines and a smaller square with straight, diagonal lines going from upper left to lower right. This smaller square aligns with the left corner of the larger square. In the top right box, we see the same 2 squares, but what has changed? The smaller square is now aligned with the right corner of the larger square (instead of the left corner).

Also, the diagonal lines have changed. They are going from lower left to upper right. The larger square has not changed. The rule is the smaller shape shifts from left to right and the lines inside switch directions. The larger shape does not change.
The answer where we see this rule is choice B.

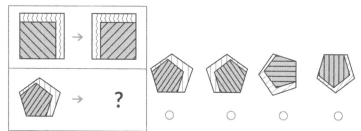

• Below are examples of basic "changes" seen in Figure Analogies.

Basic questions, like #1-#9 below, have one "change." Questions at the Grade 6 level will have at least two changes and/or changes that are not obvious. The questions in the book's two practice tests will be much more challenging than these. This is simply an intro.

1.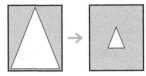

2.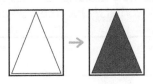

3.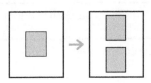

4.

5.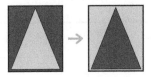

6.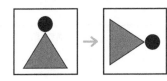

7.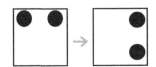

8.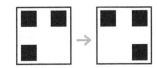

9.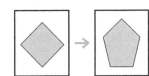

10.

1. Size (gets smaller)
2. Color (white to gray)
3. Quantity (plus 1)
4. Whole to Half
5. Color Reversal
6. Rotation (clockwise, 90°)

7. Rotation (clockwise, 90°)
8. Rotation -or- Mirror Image / "Flip"
9. Number of Shape Sides (shape with +1 side)
10. Two Changes: Rotation (clockwise, 90°) and Color Reversal

5. FIGURE CLASSIFICATION

Directions: The top row shows three pictures that are alike in some way. Look at the bottom row. There are four pictures. Which picture in the bottom row goes best with the pictures in the top row?

Explanation: Figure out a "rule" describing how the top pictures are alike and belong together. Then, apply the "rule" to each answer choice to determine which one follows it. If you find that more than one choice follows the rule, then a more specific rule is needed.

Can you come up with a rule describing how the 3 shapes are alike? They are all circles that are divided in half. In the bottom row, which choice follows this rule? Choice A is a circle, but it's not divided in half. Choice B and C are divided in half, but they are not circles. Choice D is a circle divided in half. Choice D is the answer.

Can you come up with a rule for this one? Here, in the group of 3 diamonds, there is 1 dark diamond and 2 light diamonds. Which one of the answer choices follows this rule? Choice C.

This list outlines some basic logic in Figure Classification questions. (Practice test questions will be more challenging.)

How shapes are divided (Here, shapes are divided in quarters, with 1 part filled in.)	
How many sides the shapes have (Here, it is 4.)	
Do shapes have all rounded corners or straight corners? Or, no corners at all?	
Direction shapes are facing (Here, they face right.)	
Color / Design inside shape (Here, there are dots.)	
Shape quantity in each shape group (Here, 2 shapes in each group.)	
Shape group, with a set order to the group (Here, it's circle-diamond-square.)	
Direction of inside lines (Here, diagonal from upper left to lower right side.)	

6. PAPER FOLDING

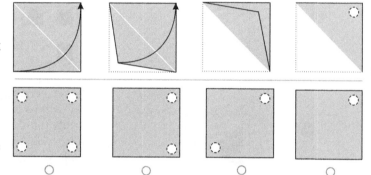

Directions: The top row of pictures shows a sheet of paper. The paper was folded, then something was cut out. Which picture in the bottom row shows how the paper would look after its unfolded?

Explanation: The first choice has too many holes. In the second choice, the holes are not in the correct position. The third choice has the correct number of holes and in the correct position. The last choice only shows the hole on top.

Tip: It is common to struggle with Paper Folding - it is not an activity most people have experience with. First, have a look at these Paper Folding examples. Then, demonstrate using real paper and scissors, if needed.

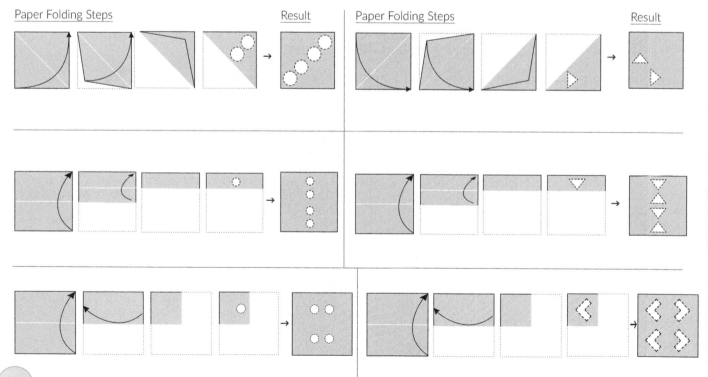

7. NUMBER SERIES (QUANTITATIVE BATTERY)

Directions: The top row of numbers have made a pattern. Which answer choice would complete the pattern?

6   9   12   15   18   <u>?</u>   A. 21   B. 3   C. 22   D. 24   E. 30

Explanation: To help see the pattern, write the difference between each number. Here, the difference between 6 and 9 is 3. The difference between 9 and 12 is 3. The difference between 12 and 15 is 3, and so on. In less challenging questions, this "difference" will be the same for each set of numbers. If the pattern is "add 3," then the answer is 21, because 18 +3 = 21. In more challenging questions, this pattern is not consistent. See below:

30	29	27	24	20	15	<u>?</u>	Pattern: -1, -2, -3, -4, etc.; Answer: 9
7	2	1	7	2	1	<u>?</u>	Pattern: 7-2-1; Answer: 7
3	4	6	7	9	10	<u>?</u>	Pattern: +1, +2, +1, +2, etc.; Answer: 12
5	0	6	0	7	0	<u>?</u>	Pattern: every other number +1; every other number=0; Ans: 8
80	160	40	80	20	40	<u>?</u>	Pattern: x2, divide by 4, x2, divide by 4, etc.; Ans: 10

8. NUMBER PUZZLES

Directions: Which number would replace the question mark so that both sides of the equal sign are the same?

Explanation: These questions have two formats. The first example is a standard math problem. In the second example, you need to replace the black shape with the given number. Should you have problems figuring out the answer of either format, you can simply test each answer choice until you find the correct answer.

1.   19 = ? + 5   A. 5   B. 24   C. 20   D. 4   E. 14

2.   ? = ■ - 8   A. 0   B. 1   C. 2   D. 3   E. 4
      ■ = 11

Note: Next is a problem with 2 variables (the square and the circle). Look at the bottom row. You can solve for the circle first. 16 - 2 = 14. So, the circle = 14. Plug 14 in for the circle in the middle row. Now, you can figure out the square. The square equals 14 + 4. So, the square is 18. Next, go to the top row and plug in 18 for the square. What is 18 ÷ 2? It is 9. So, ? = 9.

3.   ■ ÷ 2 = ?
      ■ = 4 + ●   A. 0   B. 9   C. 18   D. 6   E. 4
      ● = 16 - 2

9. NUMBER ANALOGIES

Directions: Look at the first two sets of numbers. Come up with a rule that both of these sets follow. Use this rule to figure out which answer choice goes in place of the question mark in the last set of numbers.

[2 → 6]   [4 → 12]   [10 → ?]   A. 6   B. 3   C. 13   D. 30   E. 7

Explanation: Figure out a rule that explains how the first number "changes" into the second number. It could use addition, subtraction, multiplication, or division. Write the rule by *each* pair. Make sure this rule works with *both* pairs. The rule is "multiply by 3", so 30 is the answer.

Note: There could also be 2 operations involved in the analogy. The below analogy, for example, involves multiplication as the first step and subtraction for the second step. Here, you must multiply by 2, then subtract 1. For example, in the first analogy, 2 x 2 = 4. Then, 4 -1= 3. In the second analogy, 4 x 2 = 8. Then, 8 - 1 = 7. So, 5 x 2 = 10. Then, 10 - 1 = 9. (Choice E.)

[2 → 3]   [4 → 7]   [5 → ?]   A. 6   B. 8   C. 11   D. 10   E. 9

HINTS PAGE

• COGAT® questions can be quite challenging.

• This page lists the logic (not the answers, just the logic) involved in solving some of the questions in: Verbal Classification & Analogies, Figure Classification & Analogies, and Number Analogies & Number Series.

• If this is your student's first time with COGAT® prep, you may wish to **cut out this page** and allow them to use it as they tackle these tricky questions for the first time.

Verbal Classification
1. have to do with the same thing
2. color
3. how often
4. preparation method
5. type of animal

Verbal Analogies
1. worker > material worked with
2. object > purpose
3. object > feeling
4. building > purpose
5. object > type
(Sentence: A ___ is a type of ___.)

Figure Classification
1. direction
2. shape type & position
3. number of sides
4. design inside shape
5. color of smaller shapes

Figure Analogies
1. rotation
2. shape size & color
3. color of shapes
4. position of shape
5. flip/mirror image

Number Analogies
1. subtraction
2. addition
3. multiplication

10. multiply, then add
11. multiply, then subtract
12. divide, then add

Number Series
1. multiply
2. add
3. subtract

8. multiply, then add
9. multiply, then divide
10. add, subtract, then add (a different number than the first time)

Check out our other books for COGAT® K to Grade 5

www.GatewayGifted.com

TEST-TAKING TIPS

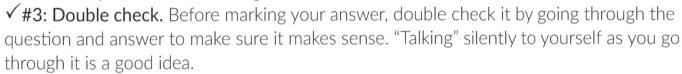

COGAT® Checklist (tips for answering questions)

✓ **#1: Do not rush.** Look carefully at the question and each answer choice.

✓ **#2: Use process of elimination.** You receive points for the number of correct answers. You will not lose points for incorrect answers. Instead of leaving a question unanswered, at least guess. First, eliminate any answers that are obviously not correct. Then, guess from those remaining.

✓ **#3: Double check.** Before marking your answer, double check it by going through the question and answer to make sure it makes sense. "Talking" silently to yourself as you go through it is a good idea.

✓ **#4: Be sure to choose only ONE answer.** When you fill in your bubble sheet, fill in only ONE bubble per question - instead of making a careless mistake and filling in two.

• Be sure to read the first section at the beginning of each group of questions in Practice Test 1. These have even more tips specific for each question type. They also have reminders to follow the "COGAT® Checklist" above.

Common Sense Tips

• **Get enough sleep.** This one is so obvious, yet so important. Studies have shown a link between not getting enough sleep and lower test scores.

• **Eat a breakfast for sustained energy and concentration.** (complex carbohydrates and protein; avoid foods/drinks high in sugar)

• **Use the restroom prior to the test.** The administrator may not allow a break during the test.

• **Don't get overly stressed.** Try not to worry about preparing for the test or the test itself. Instead, focus on doing your best. The test will have challenging questions, and sometimes, you will simply not know the answer. When this happens, instead of worrying, remain focused on answering the question the best you can and using the process of elimination (outlined above).

VERBAL CLASSIFICATION

Directions: Look at the three words on the top row. Figure out how the words are alike. Next, look at the words in the row of answer choices. Which word goes best with the three words in the top row?

Note: Try to come up with a "rule" to describe how the top three words are alike and go together. Then, take this "rule," and figure out which of the answer choices would best follow that same rule. If none of the choices work, you need to try a different rule. If more than one choice would work, then come up with a rule that is more specific. (See example below.)

- If you haven't read the Verbal Classification examples on page 5, do so now.
- Also, make sure to go through the checklist at the top of page 11.
- If you need some help with the first few, there is a "hints" section for Verbal Classification on page 10.

Example (#1): Let's start with an easy one. How do the words "start", "commence", and "kick-off" go together? What is a rule that describes how they go together?

They each have to do with beginning.

The answer would be choice D, begin. These words all have to do with the same thing.

1   **start**   **commence**   **kick off**

      Ⓐ conclude   Ⓑ present   Ⓒ direct   Ⓓ begin   Ⓔ release

2   **grass**   **lettuce**   **emerald**

      Ⓐ ruby   Ⓑ violet   Ⓒ cherry   Ⓓ butter   Ⓔ cucumber

3 **rarely** **sometimes** **frequently**

Ⓐ often Ⓑ promptly Ⓒ tardy Ⓓ overdue Ⓔ interval

4 **muffin** **cake** **pizza**

Ⓐ smoothie Ⓑ pudding Ⓒ cookie Ⓓ melon Ⓔ rice

5 **iguana** **cobra** **alligator**

Ⓐ snail Ⓑ tortoise Ⓒ shark Ⓓ frog Ⓔ caterpillar

6 **electrician** **plumber** **locksmith**

Ⓐ architect Ⓑ physician Ⓒ carpenter Ⓓ gardener Ⓔ banker

7 **barge** **forklift** **boxcar**

Ⓐ tanker truck Ⓑ limo Ⓒ sedan Ⓓ yacht Ⓔ jet ski

8 **vertical** **perpendicular** **diagonal**

Ⓐ point Ⓑ parallel Ⓒ course Ⓓ geometric Ⓔ measurement

9 **parrot** **rose** **coral**

Ⓐ teddy bear Ⓑ sand Ⓒ deer Ⓓ pebble Ⓔ oxygen

10 **microwave** **dryer** **radiator**

Ⓐ sink Ⓑ freezer Ⓒ appliance Ⓓ washer Ⓔ toaster

11 **augment** **boost** **amplify**

Ⓐ divide Ⓑ maintain Ⓒ constant Ⓓ multiply Ⓔ diminish

12 esophagus   stomach   large intestines

    Ⓐ heart   Ⓑ nose   Ⓒ lungs   Ⓓ mouth   Ⓔ blood

13 halt   cease   suspend

    Ⓐ discontinue   Ⓑ conserve   Ⓒ protect   Ⓓ warn   Ⓔ intersect

14 Mexican   Japanese   German

    Ⓐ Arabian   Ⓑ Russian   Ⓒ Asian   Ⓓ Western   Ⓔ Alaskan

15 surgeon   pharmacist   dentist

    Ⓐ nurse   Ⓑ reporter   Ⓒ mechanic   Ⓓ carpenter   Ⓔ attorney

16 honey   butter   steak

    Ⓐ ketchup   Ⓑ egg   Ⓒ onion   Ⓓ soda   Ⓔ bread

17 towering   petite   miniature

    Ⓐ munchkin   Ⓑ sheer   Ⓒ soaring   Ⓓ transparent   Ⓔ solid

18 sack   suitcase   satchel

    Ⓐ strap   Ⓑ carton   Ⓒ barrel   Ⓓ backpack   Ⓔ shuttle

19 anxious   content   elated

    Ⓐ exhausted   Ⓑ damaged   Ⓒ confident   Ⓓ prying   Ⓔ active

20 alliance   partnership   coalition

    Ⓐ union   Ⓑ member   Ⓒ independence   Ⓓ separation   Ⓔ identical

VERBAL ANALOGIES

Directions: Look at the first set of words. They go together in some way. Next, look at the second set. Then, look at the answer choices. Which answer choice goes with the word in the second set in the same way that the first set of words goes together?

Notes: Here are two strategies for tackling verbal analogies:
• Strategy 1: Come up with a "rule" to describe how the first set is related. Then, take this "rule," use it together with the second set and figure out which of the answer choices would follow that same rule. For answer choices that do not follow it, eliminate them. If more than one choice would follow it, then come up with a rule that is more specific.
• Strategy 2: Think of a sentence that describes how the first set is related. Then, complete the same process you completed with the "rule". Apply the sentence to the answer choices. Eliminate those that do not work with the sentence. If more than one choice would work, then come up with a sentence that is more specific.
• With both strategies, you may need a different rule/sentence if the first one doesn't work. (See below.)
• If you haven't read through the Verbal Analogies examples on page 5, do so now.
• If you need some help with the first few, there is a "hints" section for Verbal Analogies on page 10.

Example (#1): How do "florist" and "flowers" go together? What "rule" or sentence could describe how they go together? *Rule: The first word (florist) works with the second word (flowers). Sentence: Florists work with flowers.* Using this logic, however, creates a problem because we see that more than one answer choice could work. So, we need to be more specific. *Rule: The job of the first word (florist) involves working with a material, the second object (flowers), to create a finished product. Sentence: Florists work with flowers to create a finished product.* Now, let's see which of the answer choices work with this rule and sentence. *Sculptors work with clay to create a finished product.* The answer is D (clay).

1   **florist > flowers : sculptor > ?**

ⓐ museum   ⓑ statues   ⓒ hands   ⓓ clay   ⓔ studio

2   **life jacket > float : seat belt > ?**

ⓐ lock   ⓑ fasten   ⓒ restrain   ⓓ block   ⓔ increase

3   **silk > smooth : stone > ?**

ⓐ hard   ⓑ opaque   ⓒ gray   ⓓ rocky   ⓔ mined

4   **temple > worship : theatre > ?**

ⓐ auditorium   ⓑ applaud   ⓒ sit   ⓓ watch   ⓔ performance

5   **engineer > profession : fortress > ?**

    Ⓐ moat   Ⓑ structure   Ⓒ kingdom   Ⓓ fortify   Ⓔ battle

6   **symphony > composer : blueprint > ?**

    Ⓐ carpenter   Ⓑ roofer   Ⓒ design   Ⓓ printer   Ⓔ architect

7   **scorching > hot : ecstatic > ?**

    Ⓐ happy   Ⓑ overjoyed   Ⓒ jubilant   Ⓓ melancholy   Ⓔ distraught

8   **loud > thunderous : destructive > ?**

    Ⓐ harmful   Ⓑ cautious   Ⓒ devastating   Ⓓ damaging   Ⓔ overflowing

9   **notes > melody : steps > ?**

    Ⓐ stair   Ⓑ stride   Ⓒ shortcut   Ⓓ trek   Ⓔ destination

10   **teacher > educate : scientist > ?**

    Ⓐ fabricate   Ⓑ distort   Ⓒ educator   Ⓓ research   Ⓔ falsify

11   **peace > war : silence > ?**

    Ⓐ library   Ⓑ prayer   Ⓒ noise   Ⓓ tranquil   Ⓔ meditation

12   **milk > cow : sap > ?**

    Ⓐ bee   Ⓑ horse   Ⓒ maple syrup   Ⓓ tree   Ⓔ resin

13   **cacti > desert : bison > ?**

    Ⓐ tundra   Ⓑ swamp   Ⓒ prairie   Ⓓ herd   Ⓔ alpine

14   lava > molten :   perfume > ?

    (A) fragrant   (B) powder   (C) extract   (D) sample   (E) mixture

15   flashlight > lighthouse : paintbrush > ?

    (A) museum   (B) pen   (C) paper   (D) easel   (E) paint roller

16   glass > shard : wood > ?

    (A) splinter   (B) log   (C) lumber   (D) board   (E) tree

17   perpetual > temporary : substantial > ?

    (A) erratic   (B) whimsical   (C) evident   (D) solid   (E) meager

18   ardent > fervent: serene > ?

    (A) tranquil   (B) raucous   (C) indifferent   (D) flat   (E) tense

19   darkness > light : chaos > ?

    (A) riot   (B) order   (C) confusion   (D) disarray   (E) schedule

20   still > movement : impeccable > ?

    (A) appearance   (B) pristine   (C) invaluable   (D) fault   (E) worthless

21   skilled > expertise : educated > ?

    (A) tuition   (B) organized   (C) memory   (D) technology   (E) knowledge

22   infinite > finite : general > ?

    (A) broad   (B) degenerate   (C) common   (D) regenerate   (E) specific

SENTENCE COMPLETION

Directions: First, read the sentence. There is a missing word. Next, look at the row of answer choices below the sentence. Which word would go best in the sentence?

(Note that in some sentences there is only one word missing, and you only need to choose one word. However, in others there are two words missing, and you must choose two words.)

Notes:
- Make sure to read the <u>entire</u> sentence very carefully. To ensure you have not accidentally skipped words or misread them, we suggest "mouthing" the words to yourself. You may even want to read the sentence twice.

- Eliminate answer choices that are clearly incorrect.

- Before making your final choice, read the entire sentence again using the word(s) of your answer choice. Ask yourself if these word(s) make sense in the sentence. Ask yourself if they are the best choice.

- If you have a sentence that requires two words, make sure <u>both</u> words make sense in the sentence and that they are the best choice.

1   **The natural beauty of the landscape is an important _____ for attracting tourists.**

    Ⓐ obstacle   Ⓑ asset   Ⓒ flaw   Ⓓ barrier   Ⓔ festivity

2   **When it comes to dessert, she has a clear _____ for chocolate over vanilla.**

    Ⓐ preference   Ⓑ dessert   Ⓒ avoidance   Ⓓ disfavor   Ⓔ aroma

3   The _____ equipment must be stored separately in a special padded container.

     Ⓐ durable   Ⓑ sturdy   Ⓒ hardy   Ⓓ worthless   Ⓔ fragile

4   The breakthrough technology will _____ the field of medical research.

     Ⓐ hinder   Ⓑ delay   Ⓒ obstruct   Ⓓ advance   Ⓔ experiment

5   Since the climate was particularly _____, the region supported very little plant or animal life.

     Ⓐ arid   Ⓑ humid   Ⓒ temperate   Ⓓ unexplored   Ⓔ uncultivated

6   The committee presented two _____ proposals for the new project, each with differing advantages.

     Ⓐ similar   Ⓑ unique   Ⓒ synched   Ⓓ identical   Ⓔ duplicate

7   **Despite his extensive training, the athlete felt a surge of _____ before the game.**

Ⓐ confidence   Ⓑ determination   Ⓒ apprehension   Ⓓ positivity   Ⓔ self-assurance

8   **The medicine _____ reduced the patient's symptoms, leading to a fast recovery.**

Ⓐ slightly   Ⓑ significantly   Ⓒ marginally   Ⓓ accidentally   Ⓔ unintentionally

9   **The crowd became _____ after the concert was delayed for several hours.**

Ⓐ melodic   Ⓑ euphoric   Ⓒ upbeat   Ⓓ gracious   Ⓔ agitated

10   **The movie generated significant _____, despite receiving bad reviews from critics.**

Ⓐ losses   Ⓑ revenue   Ⓒ debt   Ⓓ aversion   Ⓔ apathy

11 To _____ a debate, we must first understand the _____ of each side's argument.

ⓐ attend, ⓑ analyze, ⓒ observe, ⓓ assess, ⓔ evaluate,
accent   harmony   volume   foundation   repetition

12 To prevent a conflict from _____, it is crucial to address the issues _____.

ⓐ worsening, ⓑ tragedy, ⓒ growing, ⓓ starting, ⓔ intensifying,
leisurely   accidentally   aimlessly   lethargically   promptly

13 "When you swim at this part of the beach, you must watch out for the _____ current," Joey's triathlon coach _____ him.

ⓐ unpredictable, ⓑ paltry, ⓒ feeble, ⓓ humid, ⓔ threatening,
urged   implored   cautioned   begged   hinted at

14 When the musicians started playing, the _____ melody filled the auditorium, which _____ the audience's spirits.

ⓐ despondent, ⓑ jubilant, ⓒ cheerful, ⓓ imperceptible, ⓔ aggravating,
elevated   invigorated dampened   enlivened   lifted

15 To _____ that the last slides stood out, she used a _____ font for the final ones.

ⓐ avoid, ⓑ prevent, ⓒ assure, ⓓ ensure, ⓔ guarantee,
animated   vivid   imperceptible   distinct   subtle

16   The book's plot was enriched by the inclusion of _____ twists and _____ characters.

     (A) unexpected, complex   (B) predictable, disagreeable   (C) anticipated, simple   (D) scarce, mundane   (E) puzzling, bewildering

17   To _____ a healthy lifestyle, it is _____ to eat a balanced diet and exercise regularly.

     (A) demonstrate, voluntary   (B) forgo, prescribed   (C) prolong, reckless   (D) establish, optional   (E) maintain, essential

18   The citizens _____ in the city square to commemorate holidays, seeing the events as fun _____.

     (A) congregate, occasions   (B) languish, spectacles   (C) dwindle, celebrations   (D) protest, misfortunes   (E) converge, tribulations

19   Even though chili peppers are _____ in Indian cuisine, they did not _____ in India.

     (A) limited, cultivate   (B) rare, develop   (C) common, originate   (D) spicy, irrigate   (E) flavorful, disperse

20   Because the official exhibited _____ in handling the dispute, her decision was _____.

     (A) objectivity, discarded   (B) bias, appealed   (C) favoritism, accepted   (D) neglect, approved   (E) hostility, hospitable

FIGURE CLASSIFICATION

Directions: Look at the three pictures on the top row. Figure out how the pictures are alike. Next, look at the pictures in the row of answer choices. Which picture goes best with the three pictures in the top row?

Note: As you did with Verbal Classification questions, together, try to come up with a "rule" to describe how the top pictures are alike and go together. Then, take this "rule," and figure out which of the answer choices would best follow that same rule. If more than one choice follows the rule, then come up with a rule that is more specific.

- Common "rules" include (but are not limited to):
  - number of sides
  - quantity
  - figure order
  - location of shape/shapes
  - rotation or direction:
    - clockwise vs. counterclockwise
    - what degree (45°, 90°, 180°)
    - "flip"/mirror image
  - color/design
  - size of figure / figure's parts
  - rounded vs. angled corners

- If you haven't read the Figure Classification examples on page 7, do so now.
- If you need some help with the first few, there is a "hints" page on page 10.

Example (#1): How do these 3 shapes go together? What is a rule that describes how they go together? They are all triangles. However, each of the answer choices is a triangle, so that can't be it.

They do not have the same inside "design" because one of the shapes is gray, one has wavy lines, and one has dots. They are different sizes. So, that can't be it either.

They are all pointing to the left. Check the answer choices. There is only 1 choice, E, that points to the left. The answer is E.

1

(A)   (B)   (C)   (D)   (E)

2

Ⓐ   Ⓑ   Ⓒ   Ⓓ   Ⓔ

3

Ⓐ   Ⓑ   Ⓒ   Ⓓ   Ⓔ

4

Ⓐ   Ⓑ   Ⓒ   Ⓓ   Ⓔ

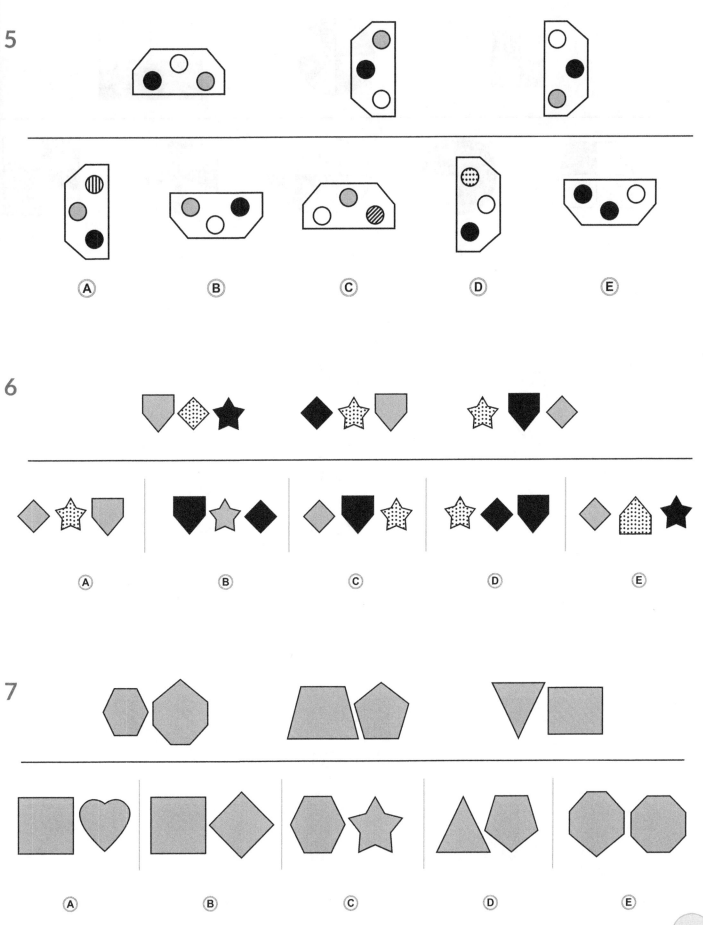

5

6

7

8

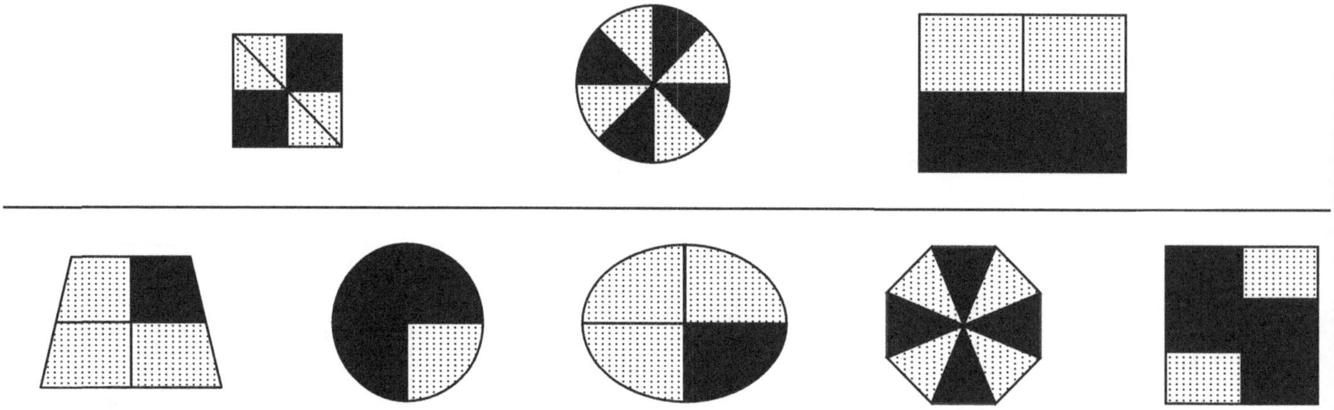

(A) (B) (C) (D) (E)

9

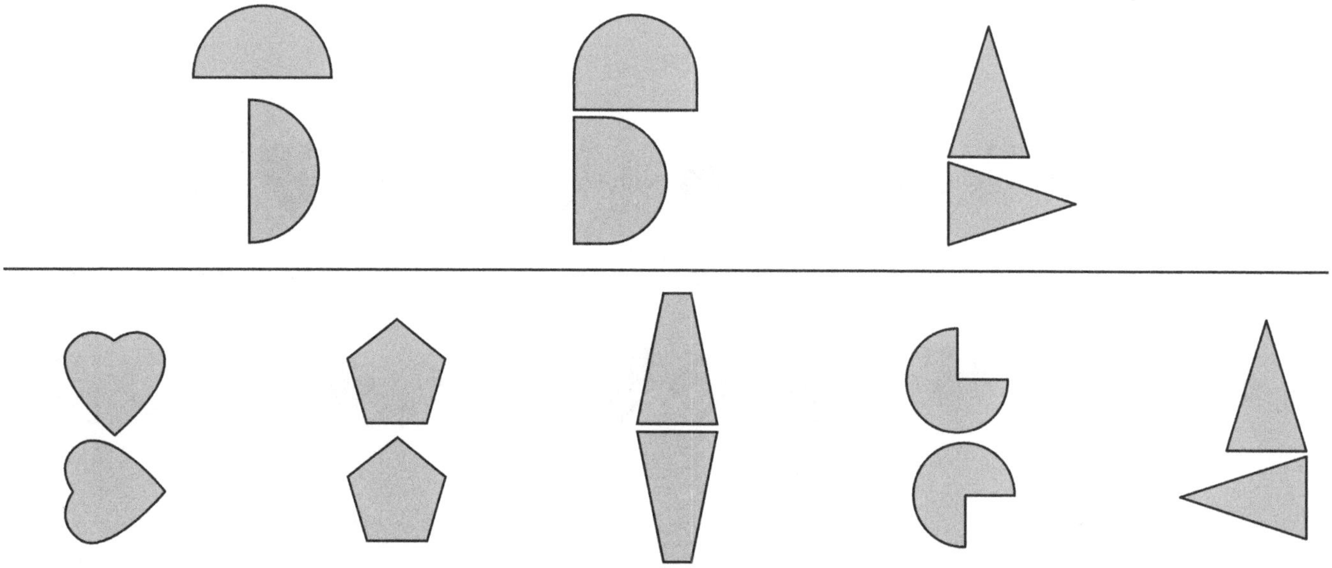

(A) (B) (C) (D) (E)

10

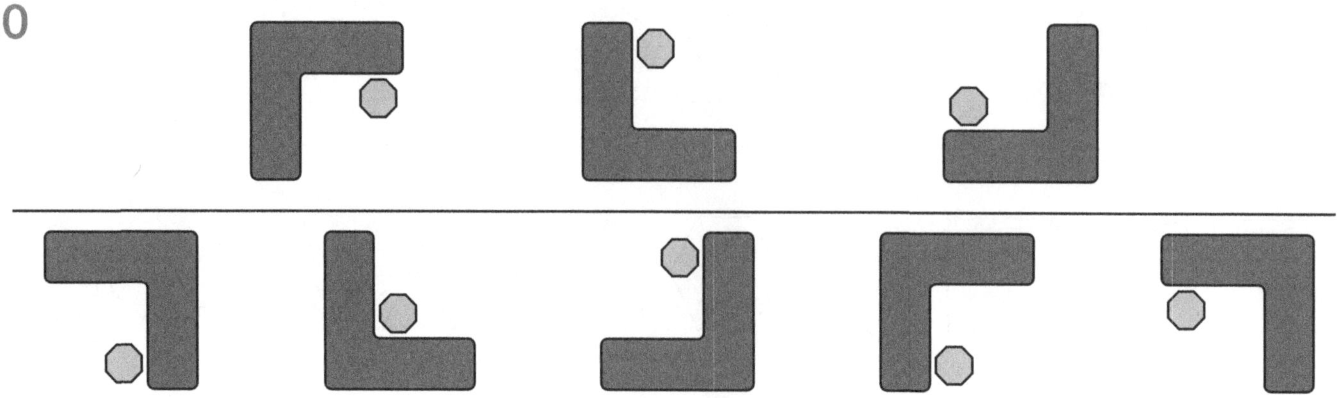

(A) (B) (C) (D) (E)

11

  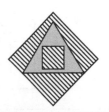

Ⓐ   Ⓑ   Ⓒ   Ⓓ   Ⓔ

12

Ⓐ   Ⓑ   Ⓒ   Ⓓ   Ⓔ

13

Ⓐ   Ⓑ   Ⓒ   Ⓓ   Ⓔ

27

14

15

16

17

18

19

A   B   C   D   E

FIGURE ANALOGIES

Directions: Look at the top set of pictures. These belong together in some way. Next, look at the bottom picture. Then, decide which answer choice would make the bottom set of pictures go together in the same way as the top set. (The small arrow shows that the set goes together.)

Note: Use the same methodology here as Verbal Analogies. Together, come up with a "rule" to describe how the first set is related. (Tip: Try to see what "changes" from the first picture to the second picture.) Then, in the second set, look at the first picture. Take this "rule," use it together with the first picture in the second set, and figure out which of the answer choices follows it. If more than one choice follows this rule, then come up with a rule that is more specific.

• You will see similar "rules" with Figure Analogies as with Figure Classification (see p.23). As with Figure Classification, these rules will often involve more than one element. If you haven't yet read this section on p.23, do so now.

• If you haven't read the Figure Analogies examples on page 6 & page 7, do so now.

• If you need some help with the first few Figure Analogies, there is a "hints" page on page 10.

• The Answer Key explanations include additional brief explanations of "rules"/"changes".

Example (#1): In the top left box, we see a diamond that has been divided into 4 equal sections. Three of those sections are light gray and 1 is dark gray. In the top right box, we see the same figure, but what has changed?

The dark section has moved. We need to figure out how it moves. It moves clockwise by 1 section.

The rule is the dark section moves clockwise by 1 section. The answer where we see this rule is B.

Be sure to pay close attention to the direction of rotation & the degree of rotation. Choice C also shows a rotation, but it is not correct.

1

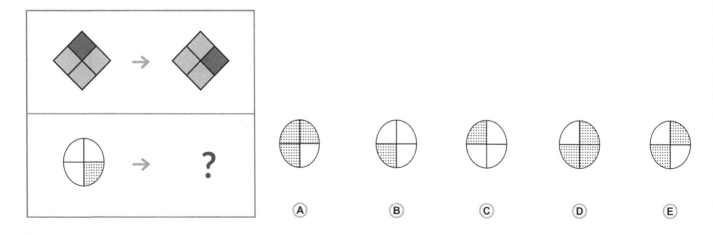

2

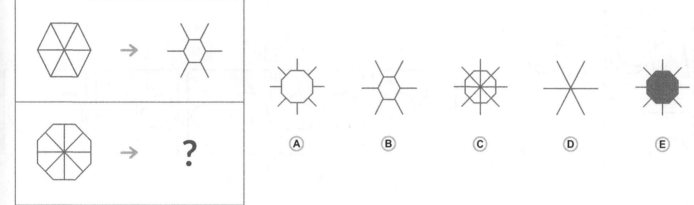

3

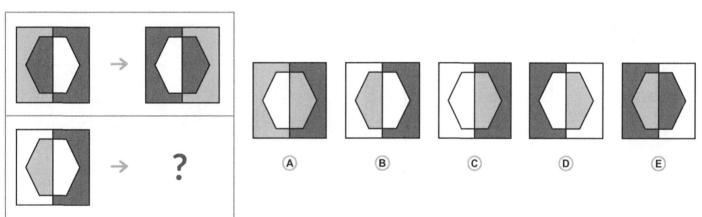

4

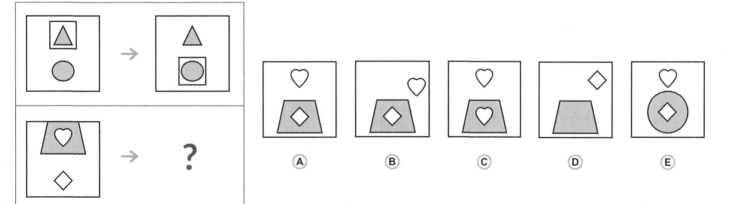

5

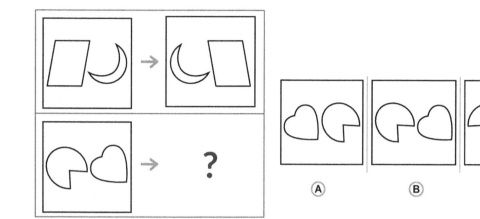

6

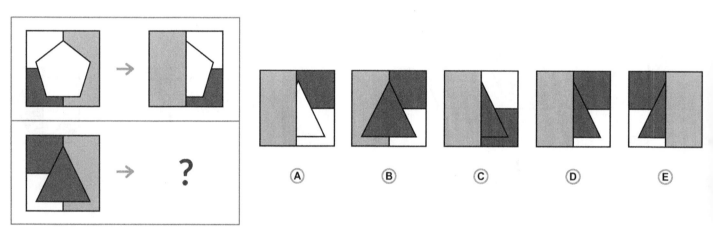

7

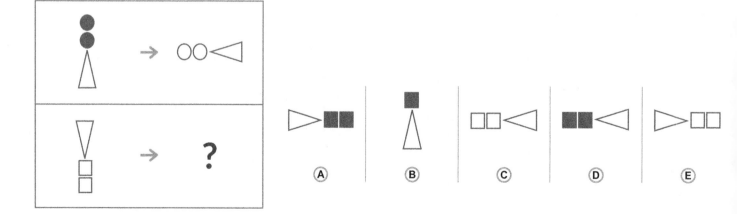

8

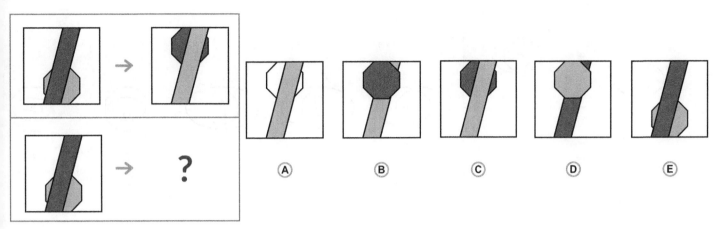

9

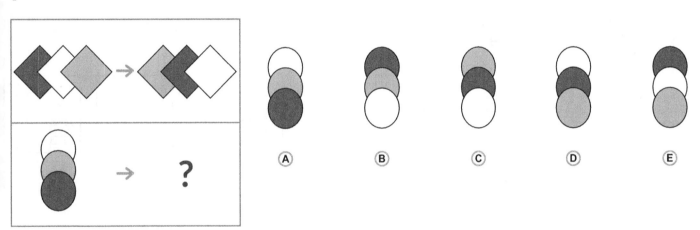

10

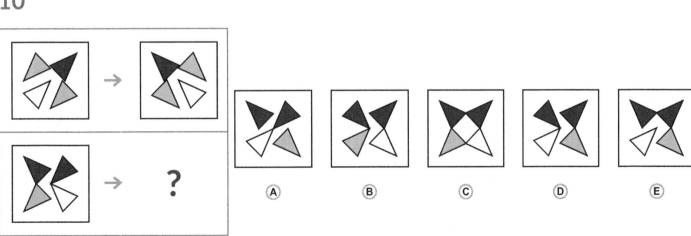

11

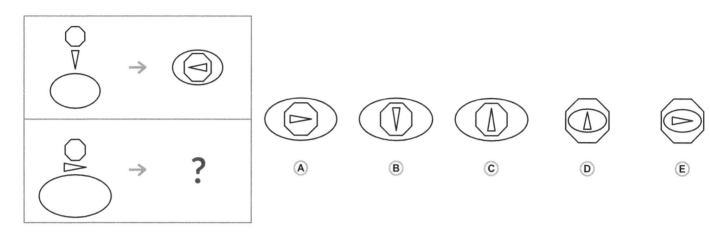

12

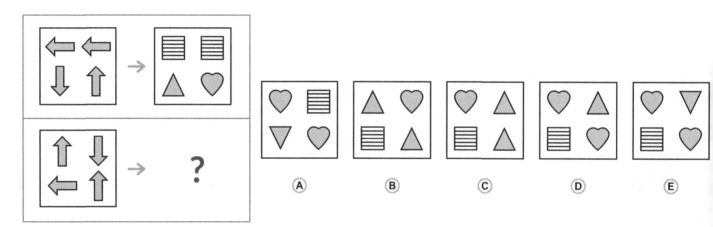

13

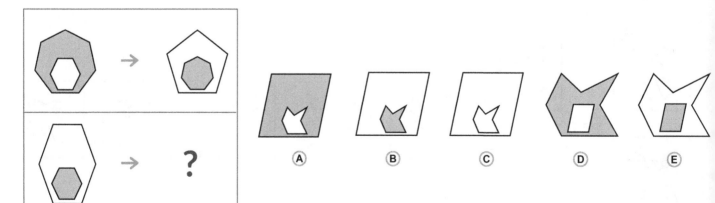

14

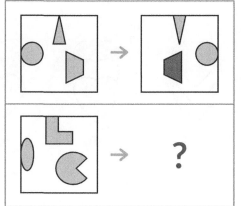

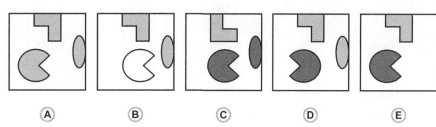

Ⓐ   Ⓑ   Ⓒ   Ⓓ   Ⓔ

15

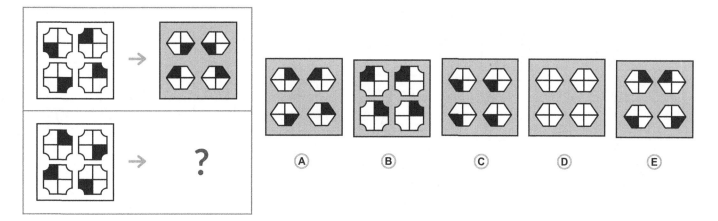

16

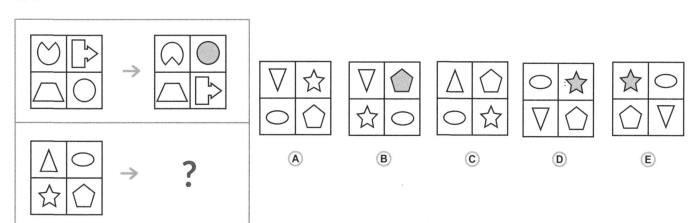

17

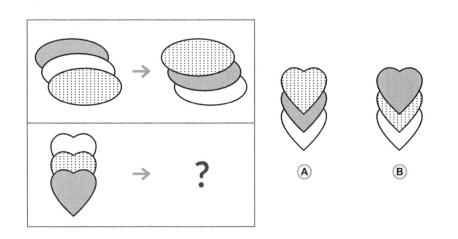

18

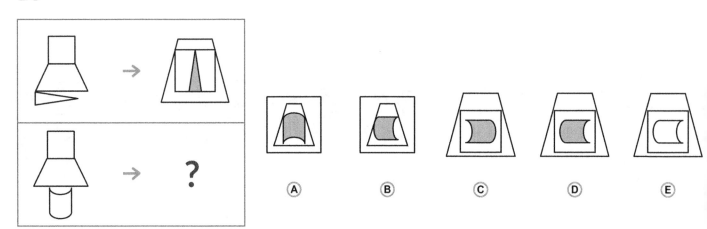

19

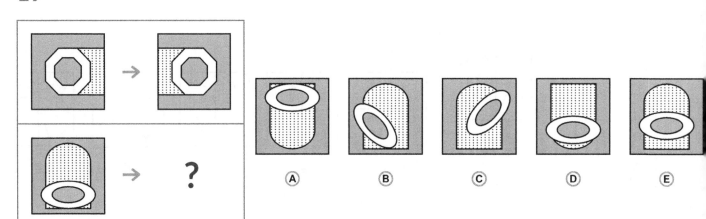

PAPER FOLDING

Directions: The top row of pictures shows a sheet of paper, how it was folded, and then how holes were made in it. Which picture on the bottom row shows how the paper would look after it is unfolded?

Note: To better understand the Paper Folding exercises, you may wish to use real paper and a hole puncher (or scissors). Be sure to notice:

- the number of times the paper is folded (for example, beginning with #3, some questions show paper folded more than once)

- the hole placement

- the number of holes made in the paper

1

 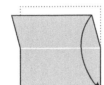 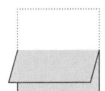

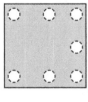   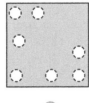 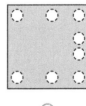 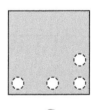

    Ⓐ   Ⓑ   Ⓒ   Ⓓ   Ⓔ

2

 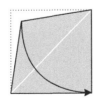  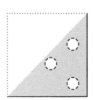

      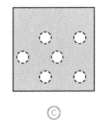 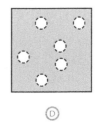 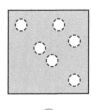

    Ⓐ   Ⓑ   Ⓒ   Ⓓ   Ⓔ

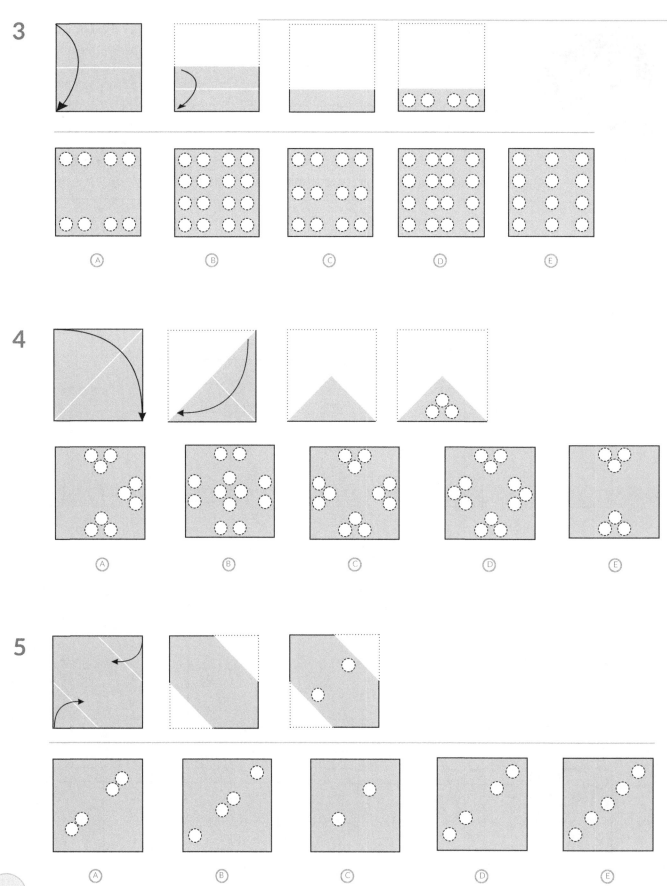

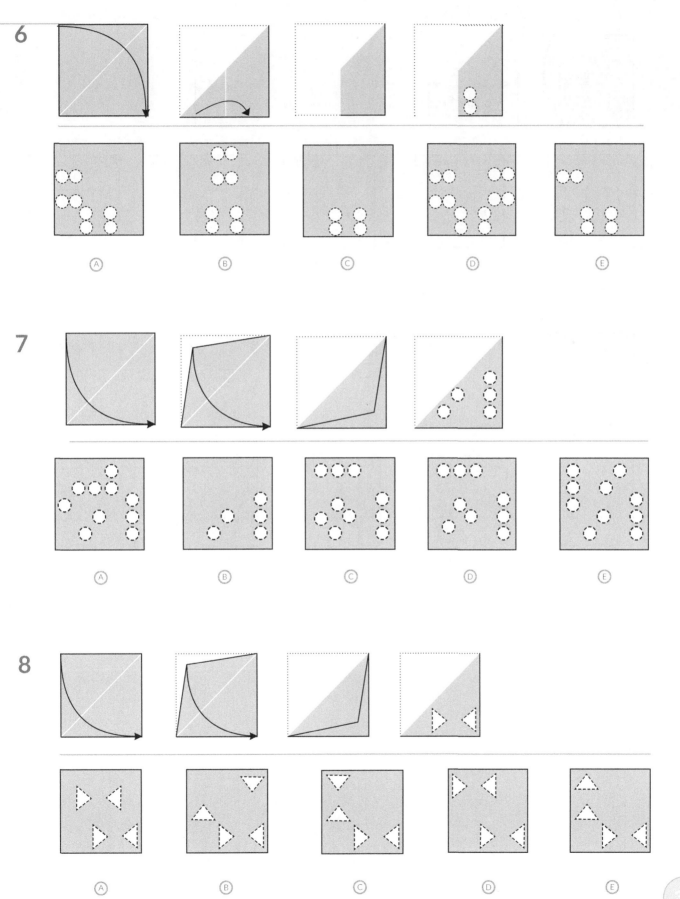

6

A B C D E

7

A B C D E

8

A B C D E

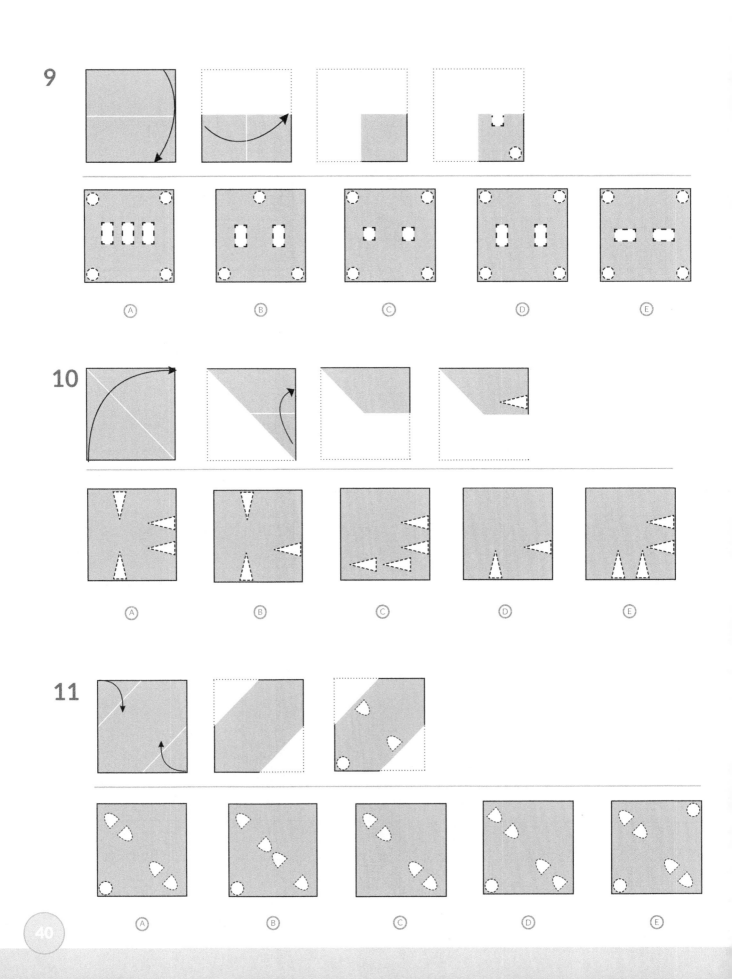

9

    Ⓐ   Ⓑ   Ⓒ   Ⓓ   Ⓔ

10

    Ⓐ   Ⓑ   Ⓒ   Ⓓ   Ⓔ

11

    Ⓐ   Ⓑ   Ⓒ   Ⓓ   Ⓔ

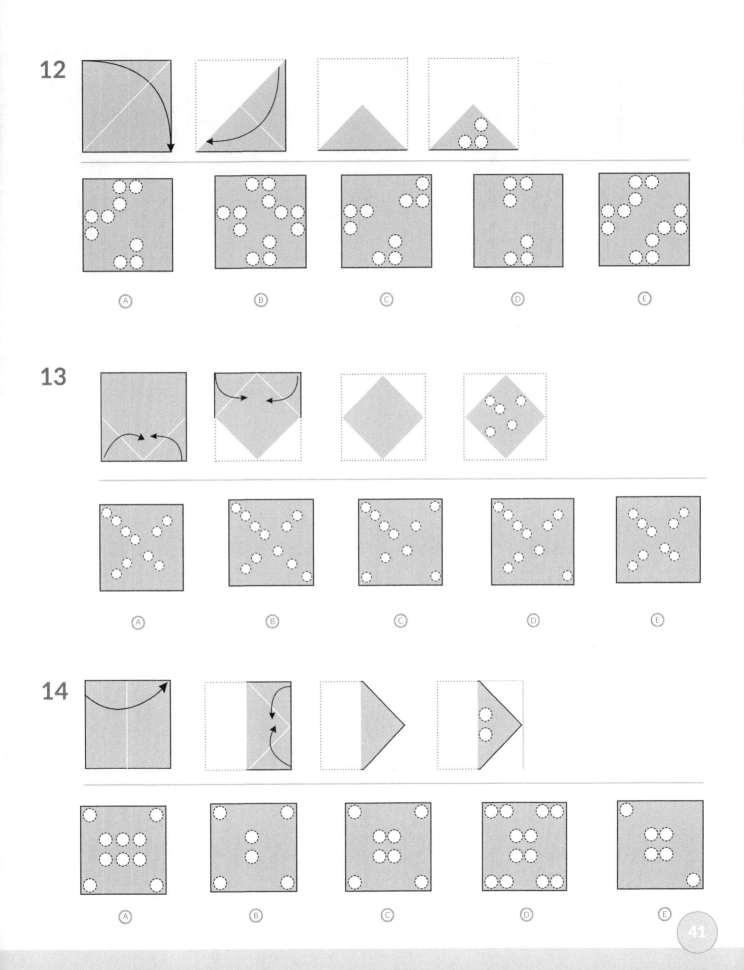

12

A   B   C   D   E

13

A   B   C   D   E

14

A   B   C   D   E

15

Ⓐ   Ⓑ   Ⓒ   Ⓓ   Ⓔ

16

Ⓐ   Ⓑ   Ⓒ   Ⓓ   Ⓔ

17

Ⓐ   Ⓑ   Ⓒ   Ⓓ   Ⓔ

NUMBER PUZZLES

Directions: What answer choice should you put in the place of the question mark so that both sides of the equal sign total the same amount?

Note: As with math problems commonly seen in school, pay close attention to the signs. Do not make the simple mistake of performing the wrong operation (i.e., adding when you should actually be subtracting). Some questions have different operations (i.e., subtracting and division).

Double check your work by replacing the question mark with your answer.

• If you haven't read the Number Puzzles examples on page 9, do so now.

Example 1: The right side of the equal sign has 145. Which answer choice do you need to put in the place of the question mark so that the left side of the equal sign is also 145? We must add 30 to 145. We get 175. 175 - 30 = 145, So, the answer is 175. Answer C is correct.

1   **? - 30 = 145**

    Ⓐ 145   Ⓑ 115   Ⓒ 175   Ⓓ 4.83   Ⓔ 185

2   **120 = 15 x ?**

    Ⓐ 7   Ⓑ 8   Ⓒ 9   Ⓓ 105   Ⓔ 135

3 $? + \blacksquare = 20$

$\blacksquare = 5$

Ⓐ 4   Ⓑ 20   Ⓒ 5   Ⓓ 10   Ⓔ 15

4 $? \times \blacksquare = 45$

$\blacksquare = 9$

Ⓐ 36   Ⓑ 54   Ⓒ 5   Ⓓ 10   Ⓔ 9

5 $? \div \blacksquare = 20$

$\blacksquare = 14$

Ⓐ 280   Ⓑ 34   Ⓒ 14   Ⓓ 6   Ⓔ 300

6 $6 + ?/4 = 6 + 0.75$

Ⓐ 4   Ⓑ 3   Ⓒ 1   Ⓓ 7   Ⓔ 2

7 $? \times \blacksquare = 45$

$9 - \blacksquare = 4$

Ⓐ 9   Ⓑ 13   Ⓒ 54   Ⓓ 36   Ⓔ 5

8 $? \times \blacksquare = 42$

   $12 - \blacksquare = 5$

(A) 7   (B) 30   (C) 8   (D) 6   (E) 17

9 $\blacksquare - 6 = ? \times 2$

   $\blacksquare = 16 \div 2$

(A) 12   (B) 4   (C) 1   (D) 8   (E) 2

10 $? - \blacksquare = 60$

   $15 - \blacksquare = 5 + 7$

(A) 12   (B) 87   (C) 27   (D) 63   (E) 72

11 $? = 30 + \blacksquare$

   $\blacksquare = 8 \times 12$

(A) 96   (B) 126   (C) 50   (D) 138   (E) 20

12 $? \times \blacksquare = 54$

   $10 - \blacksquare = 4$

(A) 54   (B) 14   (C) 15   (D) 6   (E) 9

13 ■ $\div$ 3 = ?

■ = 4 + ●

● = 2.5 x 2.0

(A) 6   (B) 15   (C) 9   (D) 3   (E) 5

14 ? = ■ + 7

18 = ■ - ●

● = 4

(A) 27   (B) 29   (C) 22   (D) 11   (E) 25

15 ● $\div$ 6 = ?

● = 12 + ■

■ = 2.5 x 9.6

(A) 6   (B) 8   (C) 24   (D) 3.83   (E) 23

16 ● $\div$ 6 = ?

● = 21 + ■

■ = 9 $\div$ 3

(A) 4   (B) 6   (C) 24   (D) 5.5   (E) 12

17 ● $\div$ 5 = ?

● = 12 + ■

■ = 7 $\times$ 4

(A) 15   (B) 10   (C) 28   (D) 56   (E) 8

NUMBER ANALOGIES

Directions Look at the first two sets of numbers. Come up with a rule that both of these sets follow. Take this rule to figure out which answer choice goes in the place of the question mark.

Note: As with Verbal Analogies, your child must try to come up with a "rule" to answer the question. It must work with *all* the pairs. Be sure to test it on each one. The "rule" will involve standard math operations (subtraction, addition, division, or multiplication).

Also, the more challenging questions will involve *two operations*.

With all of the Number Analogies questions (as with all questions), it is very important to double check your work to ensure each number pair (and then the answer) follows the rule.

• If you haven't read the Number Analogies examples on page 9, do so now.
• If you need some help with the Number Analogies, #1-#3 (where you use only 1 operation) and #10-#12 (where you must use 2 operations), see the "hints" page on page 10.

Example #1: In the first two sets you have 81 and 62, 58 and 39. How would you get from 81 to 62? How would you get from 58 to 39? In each, you subtract 19 from the first number. This is the "rule". Take this rule, look at the number at the beginning of the third set (47) and apply it to the bottom row of answer choices. What is the answer when you subtract 19 from 47? The answer is 28.

1   **[81 → 62]**   **[58 → 39]**   **[47 → ?]**

    ○ 66   ○ 27   ○ 19   ○ 28   ○ 49

2   **[34 → 62]**   **[19 → 47]**   **[45 → ?]**

    ○ 17   ○ 78   ○ 74   ○ 28   ○ 73

3   **[3 → 24]**   **[7 → 56]**   **[5 → ?]**

    ○ 40   ○ 13   ○ 58   ○ 15   ○ 45

4   [64 → 32]   [58 → 29]   [94 → ?]

    ○ 42   ○ 47   ○ 50   ○ 38   ○ 48

5   [13 → 169]   [14 → 196]   [15 → ?]

    ○ 30   ○ 211   ○ 225   ○ 150   ○ 250

6   [1.2 → 0.12]   [3.6 → 0.36]   [4.5 → ?]

    ○ 0.45   ○ 0.045   ○ 45   ○ 4.5   ○ 4.50

7   [24 → 2.4]   [120 → 12]   [9.7 → ?]

    ○ 97   ○ 0.97   ○ 9.7   ○ 9.70   ○ 0.097

8   [12/16 → 3/4]   [8/32 → 1/4]   [15/20 → ?]

    ○ 1/4   ○ 4/3   ○ 1/2   ○ 1/5   ○ 3/4

9   [5 → 65]   [2.5 → 32.5]   [7.8 → ?]

     ○ 10.14   ○ 0.8   ○ 1014.0   ○ 93.6   ○ 101.4

10   [4 → 9]   [7 → 15]   [10 → ?]

     ○ 22   ○ 18   ◉ 19   ○ 21   ○ 20

11   [35 → 69]   [48 → 95]   [57 → ?]

     ○ 114   ○ 113   ○ 60   ○ 61   ○ 189

12   [60 → 31]   [84 → 43]   [72 → ?]

     ○ 36   ○ 38   ○ 37   ○ 71   ○ 55

13   [21 → 65]   [26 → 80]   [24 → ?]

     ○ 74   ○ 72   ○ 75   ○ 70   ○ 95

14   [8 → 33]   [12 → 49]   [15 → ?]

○ 60   ○ 59   ○ 64   ○ 61   ○ 58

15   [12 → 144]   [16 → 256]   [18 → ?]

○ 216   ○ 288   ○ 320   ○ 360   ○ 324

16   [243 → 27]   [126 → 14]   [189 → ?]

○ 23   ○ 21   ○ 36   ○ 9   ○ 90

17   [28 → 112]   [32 → 128]   [37 → ?]

○ 41   ○ 132   ○ 146   ○ 148   ○ 152

18   [64 → 17]   [80 → 21]   [52 → ?]

○ 13   ○ 15   ○ 4   ○ 5   ○ 14

19   **245→237**   **312→304**   **489→?**

   ○ 481   ○ 497   ○ 312   ○ 480   ○ 488

20   **[75 → 26]**   **[90 → 31]**   **[84 → ?]**

   ○ 28   ○ 30   ○ 18   ○ 81   ○ 29

21   **[25 → 101]**   **[32 → 129]**   **[28 → ?]**

   ○ 120   ○ 114   ○ 112   ○ 111   ○ 113

22   **[100→21]**   **[125→26]**   **[85→?]**

   ○ 17   ○ 90   ○ 18   ○ 80   ○ 19

23   **15→49**   **22→70**   **18→?**

   ○ 75   ○ 58   ○ 54   ○ 72   ○ 70

NUMBER SERIES

Directions: Here, you must try to figure out a pattern that the numbers have made. Which answer choice would complete the pattern?

Note: As with other question types, it is helpful to figure out a "rule" that the numbers have made. In this section, it is a pattern. Use the "rule"/pattern to figure out the missing number. As with the Number Analogies, the rules will involve subtraction, addition, division, or multiplication.

Some of these are quite challenging and involve more than one "rule". They could even involve more than one kind of operation (addition/subtraction/multiplication/division).

Double check your work to ensure the series of numbers (and then the answer) follows the rule/pattern.

- If you haven't read the Number Series examples on page 9, do so now.
- If you need some help with the Number Series, #1-#3 (where you use only 1 operation) and #8-#10 (where you must use 2 operations), see the "hints" page on page 10.

Example #1: Do you see a pattern or a rule that the numbers in the series follow? How do you get from 3 to 6, then from 6 to 12, then from 12 to 24, then from 24 to 48? Each time, each number is multiplied by 2. If this is the pattern, then what would come after 48? It's Choice D, 96.

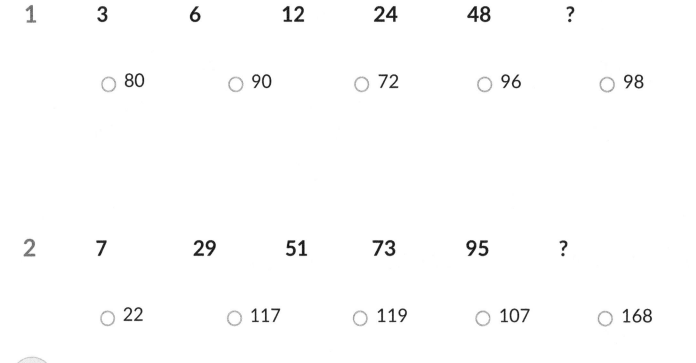

1   3   6   12   24   48   ?

   ○ 80   ○ 90   ○ 72   ○ 96   ○ 98

2   7   29   51   73   95   ?

   ○ 22   ○ 117   ○ 119   ○ 107   ○ 168

3   **230**   **192**   **154**   **116**   **78**   **?**

○ 36   ○ 42   ○ 40   ○ 38   ○ 30

4   **47**   **53**   **47**   **58**   **47**   **63**   **47**   **?**

○ 68   ○ 47   ○ 67   ○ 70   ○ 65

5   **8**   **7**   **5**   **4**   **2**   **?**

○ 3   ○ 0   ○ -1   ○ -2   ○ 1

6   **94**   **83**   **71**   **58**   **44**   **?**

○ 29   ○ 28   ○ 27   ○ 30   ○ 31

7   **45**   **46**   **47**   **49**   **50**   **51**   **53**   **54**   **?**

○ 57   ○ 56   ○ 54   ○ 55   ○ 58

8 **7**   **14**   **15**   **30**   **31**   **?**

○ 58   ○ 59   ○ 60   ○ 61   ○ 62

9 **7**   **28**   **14**   **56**   **28**   **112**   **?**

○ 224   ○ 56   ○ 448   ○ 110   ○ 24

10 **8** **11** **6** **13** **16** **11** **18** **21** **?**

○ 24   ○ 28   ○ 26   ○ 16   ○ 5

11 **50** **39** **51** **40** **52** **41** **53** **42** **?**

○ 43   ○ 44   ○ 53   ○ 54   ○ 55

12 **70** **45** **69** **46** **68** **47** **67** **48** **?**

○ 49   ○ 47   ○ 66   ○ 67   ○ 65

13 7 9 11 10 12 14 13 15 ?

○ 11   ○ 18   ○ 15   ○ 16   ○ 17

14 1 2 3 2 4 6 4 7 10 ?

○ 7   ○ 8   ○ 9   ○ 6   ○ 5

15 4 8 16 8 16 32 16 32 64 ?

○ 64   ○ 16   ○ 32   ○ 8   ○ 2

16 21 16 24 18 13 21 15 10 18 ?

○ 13   ○ 12   ○ 26   ○ 10   ○ 11

17 147 150 154 159 165 172 180 ?

○ 189   ○ 188   ○ 187   ○ 190   ○ 191

18   **151**   **-150**   **149**   **-148**   **147**   **-146**   **145**   **?**

     ○ -143   ○ 143   ○ -144   ○ -145   ○ 144

19   **12**   **11**   **10**   **10**   **8**   **9**   **6**   **?**

     ○ 9   ○ 5   ○ 6   ○ 7   ○ 8

20   **5**   **13**   **15**   **22**   **45**   **31**   **?**

     ○ 155   ○ 40   ○ 405   ○ 135   ○ 54

21   **10**   **4**   **9**   **5**   **8**   **6**   **?**

     ○ 5   ○ 6   ○ 7   ○ 8   ○ 4

22   **4**   **8**   **24**   **48**   **144**   **?**

     ○ 432   ○ 288   ○ 248   ○ 388   ○ 332

23   **40**   **37**   **41**   **36**   **30**   **37**   **29**   **20**   **30**   **?**

     ○ 19   ○ 9   ○ 12   ○ 40   ○ 21

- End of Practice Test 1. Practice Test 2 begins on the next page. -

VERBAL CLASSIFICATION, PRACTICE TEST 2 / Directions: The top row has three words that are alike in some way. On the bottom row are five words. Which word on the bottom row goes best with the words on the top row?

1   **ligament**   **tendon**   **skeleton**

Ⓐ heart   Ⓑ liver   Ⓒ pancreas   Ⓓ gland   Ⓔ cartilage

2   **transparent**   **opaque**   **translucent**

Ⓐ tremendous   Ⓑ sheer   Ⓒ massive   Ⓓ substantial   Ⓔ buoyant

3   **crimson**   **scarlet**   **burgundy**

Ⓐ amber   Ⓑ sapphire   Ⓒ ruby   Ⓓ emerald   Ⓔ gold

4   **pouch**   **safe**   **bottle**

Ⓐ drink   Ⓑ plank   Ⓒ button   Ⓓ drawer   Ⓔ mirror

5   **chicken**   **rice**   **pork**

Ⓐ carrots   Ⓑ lentils   Ⓒ berries   Ⓓ cherries   Ⓔ mushrooms

6   **scarce**   **sparse**   **scant**

Ⓐ plentiful   Ⓑ amount   Ⓒ minimal   Ⓓ primary   Ⓔ essential

7   **campus**   **degree**   **faculty**

Ⓐ curriculum   Ⓑ altar   Ⓒ audience   Ⓓ reservation   Ⓔ accommodation

8   **velvet**   **wool**   **cotton**

Ⓐ pillow   Ⓑ jacket   Ⓒ material   Ⓓ linen   Ⓔ thread

9   **root**   **basement**   **pit**

Ⓐ layer   Ⓑ foundation   Ⓒ interior   Ⓓ pinnacle   Ⓔ preliminary

10   **mystery**   **fantasy**   **science fiction**

Ⓐ poetry   Ⓑ author   Ⓒ category   Ⓓ style   Ⓔ audiobook

11   **vinegar**   **cider**   **blood**

Ⓐ air   Ⓑ diamond   Ⓒ bandage   Ⓓ apple   Ⓔ milk

12   **TV**   **tablet**   **ATM**

Ⓐ record player   Ⓑ laptop   Ⓒ mirror   Ⓓ lightbulb   Ⓔ blender

13   **trolley**   **ferry**   **cruise ship**

Ⓐ kayak   Ⓑ bus   Ⓒ motorcycle   Ⓓ scooter   Ⓔ bicycle

14   **season**   **second**   **decade**

Ⓐ birthday   Ⓑ summer   Ⓒ calendar   Ⓓ semester   Ⓔ clock

15   **ATM**   **vending machines**   **soda fountain**

Ⓐ gate   Ⓑ vault   Ⓒ fuel pump   Ⓓ microwave   Ⓔ washing machine

16   **amplify**   **augment**   **expand**

Ⓐ divide   Ⓑ deflate   Ⓒ elevate   Ⓓ permanent   Ⓔ consistent

17   **Roman**   **Mongol**   **British**

Ⓐ Ottoman   Ⓑ Canadian   Ⓒ Icelandic   Ⓓ Swiss   Ⓔ Belize

18   **appraise**   **assess**   **gauge**

Ⓐ cite   Ⓑ evaluate   Ⓒ assemble   Ⓓ arrange   Ⓔ coordinate

19   **antagonist**   **adversary**   **nemesis**

Ⓐ counterpart   Ⓑ enforcer   Ⓒ controller   Ⓓ proponent   Ⓔ foe

VERBAL ANALOGIES, PRACTICE TEST 2 / **Directions:** The first set of words goes together in some way. Which answer choice would make the second set of words go together in the same way as the first set?

1 **enormous > large : freezing > ?**

Ⓐ snowy Ⓑ ice Ⓒ temperature Ⓓ cold Ⓔ arctic

2 **heavy > weight : fast > ?**

Ⓐ speed Ⓑ quick Ⓒ race Ⓓ engine Ⓔ vehicle

3 **movies > theater : artifacts > ?**

Ⓐ quarry Ⓑ museum Ⓒ archeologist Ⓓ university Ⓔ cemetery

4 **brave > cowardly : energetic > ?**

Ⓐ vigorous Ⓑ dynamic Ⓒ energy Ⓓ strength Ⓔ lethargic

5 **spark > fire : flood > ?**

Ⓐ landslide Ⓑ rain Ⓒ tsunami Ⓓ dehydration Ⓔ storm

6 **wagon > car : typewriter > ?**

Ⓐ printer Ⓑ calculator Ⓒ computer Ⓓ cell phone Ⓔ notebook

7 **building > roof : forest > ?**

Ⓐ layer Ⓑ floor Ⓒ ecosystem Ⓓ tree Ⓔ canopy

8 **firework > explode : balloon > ?**

Ⓐ buoyant Ⓑ hover Ⓒ drift Ⓓ burst Ⓔ float

9 **pollution > environment : dishonesty > ?**

Ⓐ fraud Ⓑ plagiarism Ⓒ trust Ⓓ wealth Ⓔ affluence

10 **expand > enlarge : diminish > ?**

Ⓐ amplify Ⓑ obscure Ⓒ faded Ⓓ divide Ⓔ reduce

11 **lung > air : engine > ?**

Ⓐ vehicle Ⓑ exhaust Ⓒ water Ⓓ fuel Ⓔ heat

12 **exciting > thrilling: noteworthy > ?**

ⓐ remarkable   ⓑ surprising   ⓒ ordinary   ⓓ satisfactory   ⓔ anticipated

13 **boisterous > hushed: initiate > ?**

ⓐ continue   ⓑ conclude   ⓒ extend   ⓓ introduce   ⓔ launch

14 **neglect > care : ignorance > ?**

ⓐ attention   ⓑ knowledge   ⓒ honesty   ⓓ disbelief   ⓔ diligence

15 **storm > flood : drought > ?**

ⓐ irrigate   ⓑ desert   ⓒ arid   ⓓ monsoon   ⓔ famine

16 **flashlight > lantern : clock > ?**

ⓐ alarm   ⓑ sundial   ⓒ compass   ⓓ thermometer   ⓔ time

17 **cryptic > decipher : obstacle > ?**

ⓐ ignore   ⓑ understand   ⓒ overcome   ⓓ create   ⓔ deter

18 **vibrancy > fade : size > ?**

ⓐ contract   ⓑ enlarge   ⓒ expand   ⓓ magnify   ⓔ stabilize

19 **fresh > stale : contemporary > ?**

ⓐ new   ⓑ satisfactory   ⓒ obsolete   ⓓ immediate   ⓔ present

20 **assist > help : disclose > ?**

ⓐ reveal   ⓑ enclose   ⓒ withhold   ⓓ suppress   ⓔ deposit

21 **innocent > guilt : aimless > ?**

ⓐ time   ⓑ direction   ⓒ idle   ⓓ erratic   ⓔ random

22 **hierarchical > rank : geographical > ?**

ⓐ climate   ⓑ atlas   ⓒ age   ⓓ location   ⓔ subject

SENTENCE COMPLETION / PRACTICE TEST 2 / Directions: First, read the sentence. A word is missing. Then, look below the sentence at each of the answer choices. Which choice would go best in the sentence?

1 **As the collection increases, the museum aims to _____ rare artifacts from around the world.**

Ⓐ discard   Ⓑ obtain   Ⓒ bury   Ⓓ distort   Ⓔ consume

2 **To achieve the best performance, it is crucial to find the _____ settings for your computer.**

Ⓐ random   Ⓑ irregular   Ⓒ optimal   Ⓓ erratic   Ⓔ uncommon

3 **The two _____ solutions proposed will take you in opposite directions.**

Ⓐ contrasting   Ⓑ parallel   Ⓒ complementary   Ⓓ matching   Ⓔ coordinating

4 **Filmmakers often use dramatic music to _____ the mood of a scene.**

Ⓐ downplay   Ⓑ undermine   Ⓒ reduce   Ⓓ upset   Ⓔ enhance

5 **With the school's shift to online learning, the physical location of students has become largely _____.**

Ⓐ important   Ⓑ crucial   Ⓒ essential   Ⓓ irrelevant   Ⓔ educational

6   The garbage has become _____ after sitting in the sun all day-take it out immediately!

ⓐ rancid   ⓑ pleasant   ⓒ aromatic   ⓓ swollen   ⓔ inflated

7   As the architect is _____, she can design structures required for the project.

ⓐ novice   ⓑ inexperienced   ⓒ proficient   ⓓ naïve   ⓔ inept

8   I frequently speak up to support Mark during discussions. Mark calls me his _____.

ⓐ adversary   ⓑ ally   ⓒ bystander   ⓓ antagonist   ⓔ spectator

9   The coach held extra practices to _____ the talents of the aspiring athletes.

ⓐ cultivate   ⓑ suppress   ⓒ diminish   ⓓ recede   ⓔ exhaust

10   The fiery employee was consumed by _____ when he discovered that the promotion had been awarded to someone else.

ⓐ gratitude   ⓑ rage   ⓒ contentment   ⓓ relief   ⓔ competence

11   **Prior to first stepping on stage, the anxious musician was gripped by _____.**

(A) composure   (B) confidence   (C) lyrics   (D) refrains   (E) trepidation

12   **The Sahara Desert spans a large portion of North Africa, but it is _____ inhabited due to the _____ conditions.**

(A) densely,
mild

(B) scarcely,
harsh

(C) heavily,
favorable

(D) quite,
temperate

(E) fully,
parched

13   **The director _____ the rehearsal would go smoothly, but it was _____.**

(A) worried,
orderly

(B) predicted,
flawless

(C) assumed,
successful

(D) anticipated,
chaotic

(E) thought,
productive

14   **A weather app _____ updates by showing forecasts for _____ days.**

(A) withholds,
future

(B) conceals,
cloudy

(C) presents,
temperate

(D) automatically,
previous

(E) provides,
subsequent

15   **The national economy grew thanks to _____ resources, which fueled a _____ industrial sector.**

(A) mediocre,
robust

(B) rare,
trivial

(C) abundant,
powerful

(D) bountiful,
stagnant

(E) minimal,
shrinking

16 One challenge of deep-sea diving is that it becomes more _____ as you descend to greater _____.

    (A) placid, crests   (B) relaxing, reefs   (C) effortless, heights   (D) calm, currents   (E) strenuous, depths

17 Given the _____ talents of the team, collective work often produces _____ results.

    (A) unique, mediocre   (B) moderate, significant   (C) limited, extraordinary   (D) distinct, exceptional   (E) average, remarkable

18 Even with their best efforts, the _____ obstacle wouldn't move, no matter how they tried to _____ it."

    (A) vanish, observe   (B) entrenched, dislodge   (C) temporary, reinforce   (D) invisible, ignore   (E) pliable, broaden

19 To _____ the adverse effects of air pollution, the government _____ strict emission regulations.

    (A) mitigate, implements   (B) reduce, rejects   (C) lessen, postponed   (D) intensify, overlooks   (E) amplify, imposes

Figure Classification Directions: Which answer choice in the bottom row goes best with the 3 pictures in the top row?

1

A   B   C   D   E

2

A   B   C   D   E

3

A   B   C   D   E

4

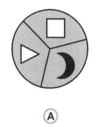 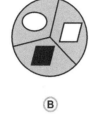 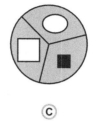 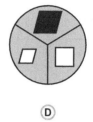 

(A)   (B)   (C)   (D)   (E)

5

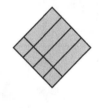 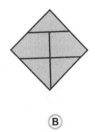  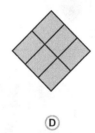 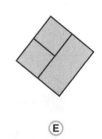

(A)   (B)   (C)   (D)   (E)

6

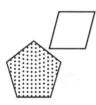 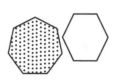 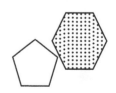

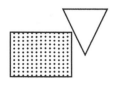 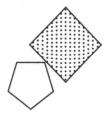  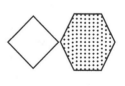 

(A)   (B)   (C)   (D)   (E)

7

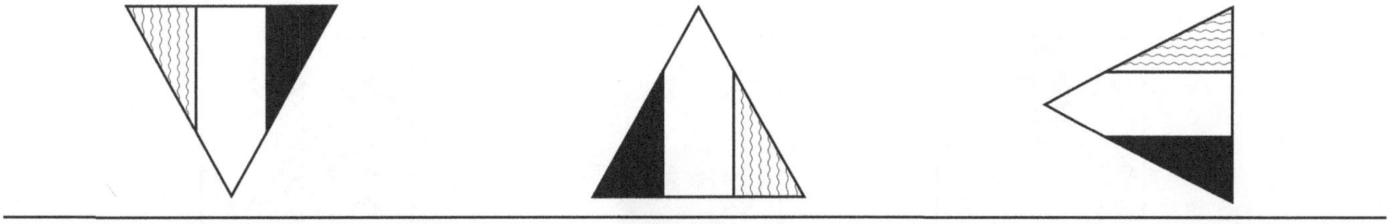

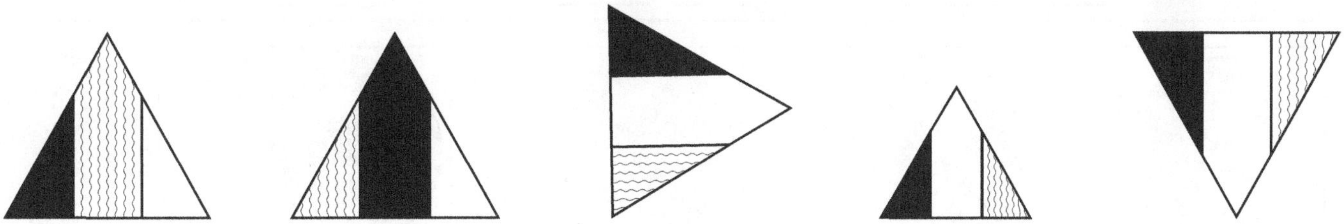

A   B   C   D   E

8

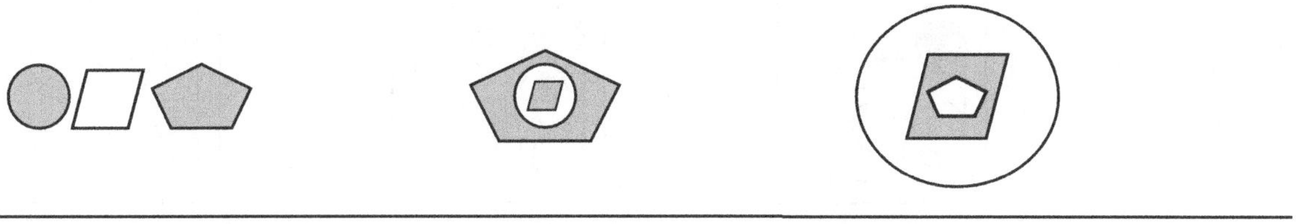

A   B   C   D   E

9

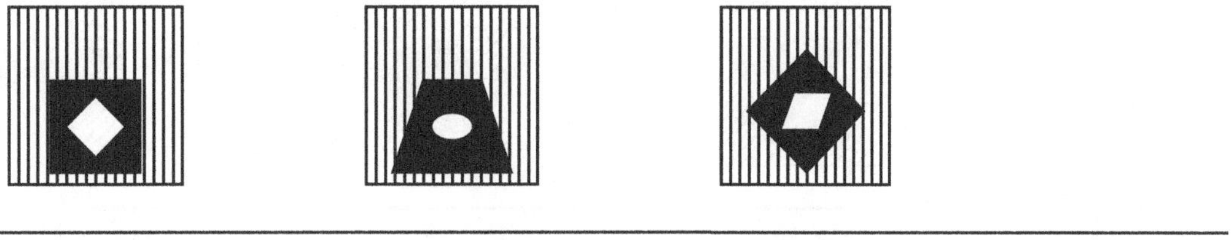

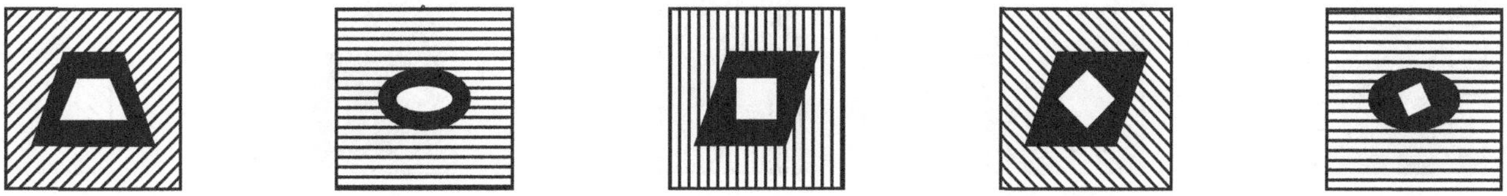

A   B   C   D   E

10

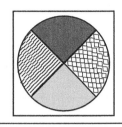 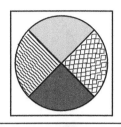 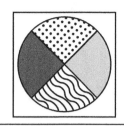

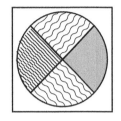 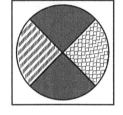 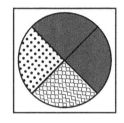 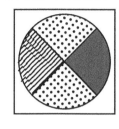

Ⓐ   Ⓑ   Ⓒ   Ⓓ   Ⓔ

11

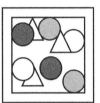  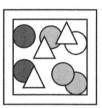

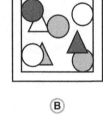 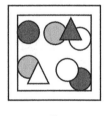 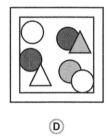 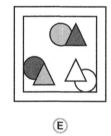

Ⓐ   Ⓑ   Ⓒ   Ⓓ   Ⓔ

12

    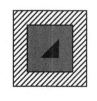

Ⓐ   Ⓑ   Ⓒ   Ⓓ   Ⓔ

13

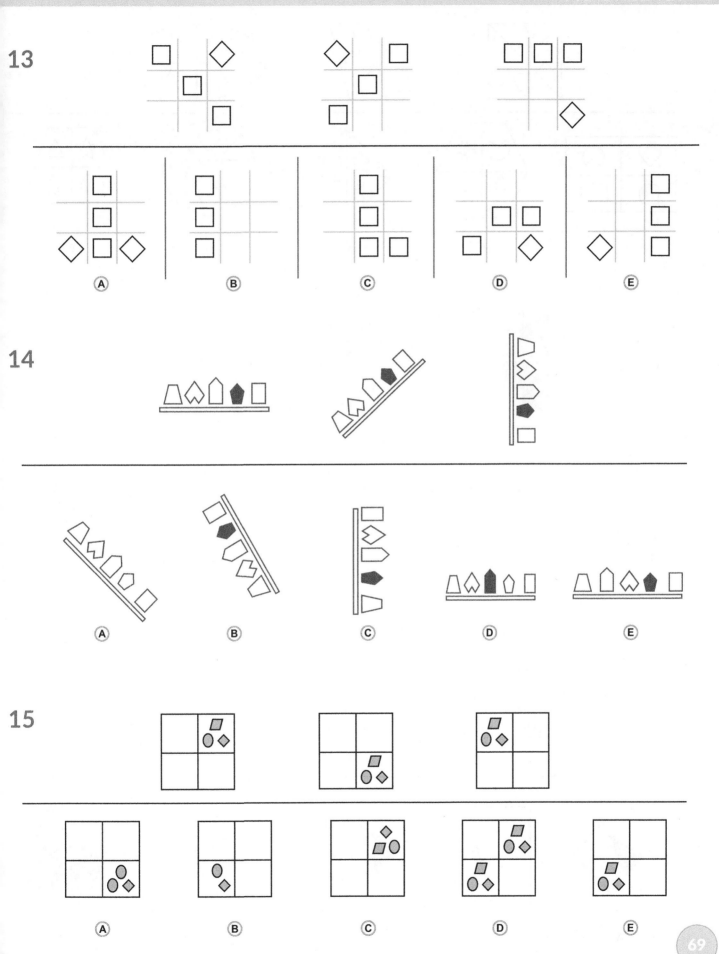

14

15

16

  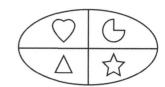

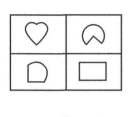   

Ⓐ   Ⓑ   Ⓒ   Ⓓ   Ⓔ

17

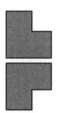  

Ⓐ   Ⓑ   Ⓒ   Ⓓ   Ⓔ

18

 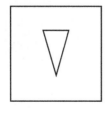   

Ⓐ   Ⓑ   Ⓒ   Ⓓ   Ⓔ

Figure Analogies Directions: Which choice makes the second set of pictures go together in the same way as the first set?

1

Ⓐ   Ⓑ   Ⓒ   Ⓓ   Ⓔ

2

Ⓐ   Ⓑ   Ⓒ   Ⓓ   Ⓔ

3

Ⓐ   Ⓑ   Ⓒ   Ⓓ   Ⓔ

4

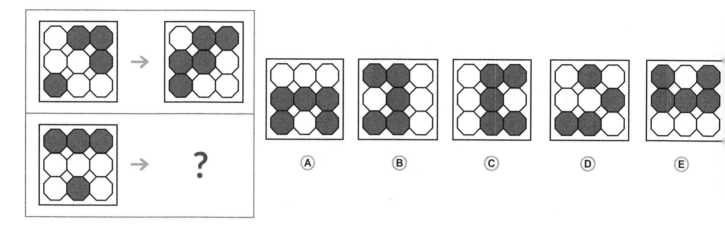

5

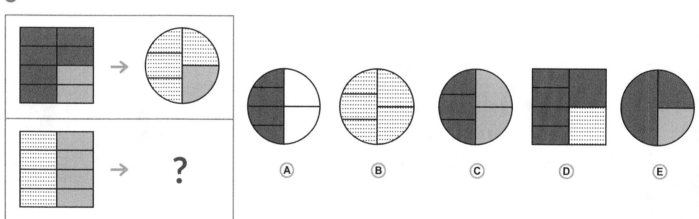

6

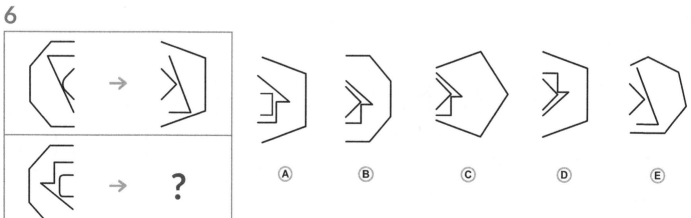

7

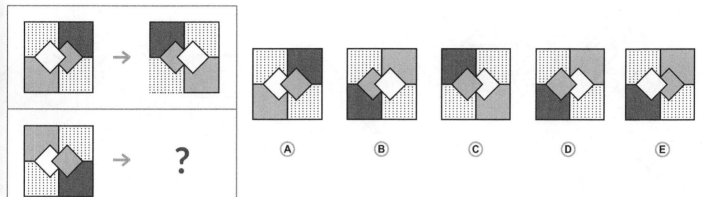

8

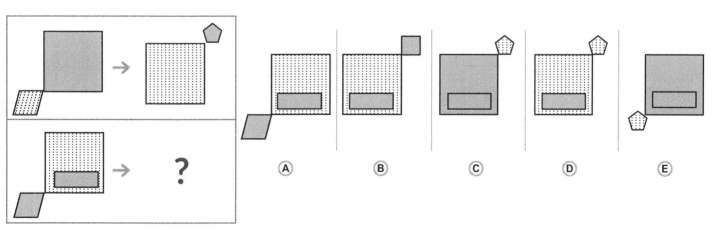

9

10

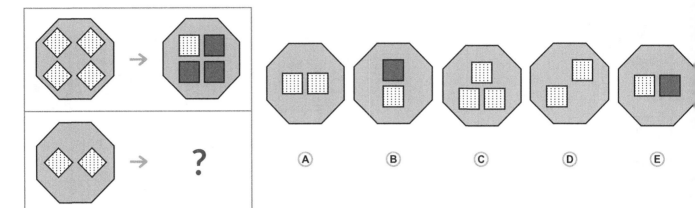

11

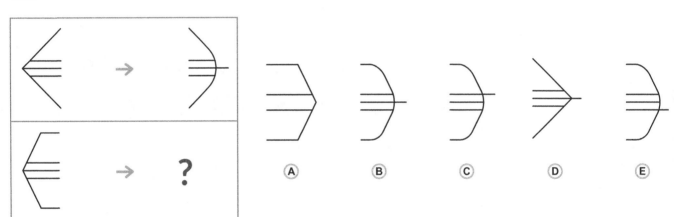

12

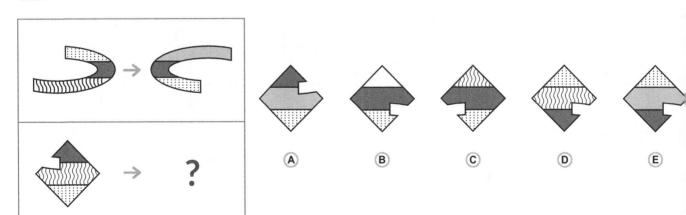

13

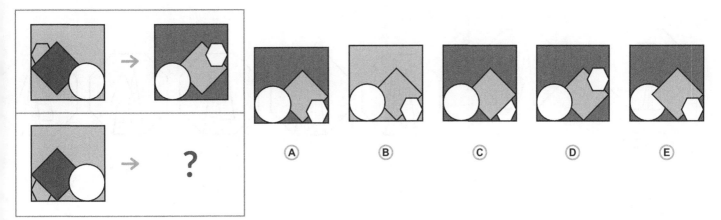

14

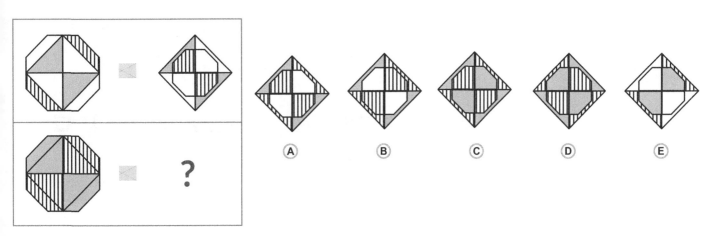

15

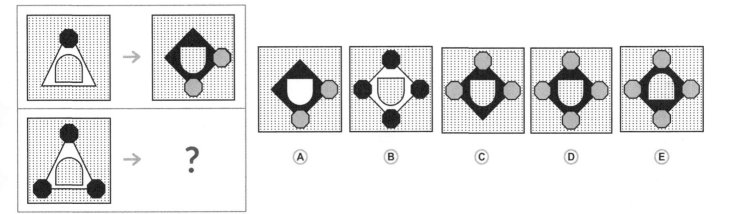

16

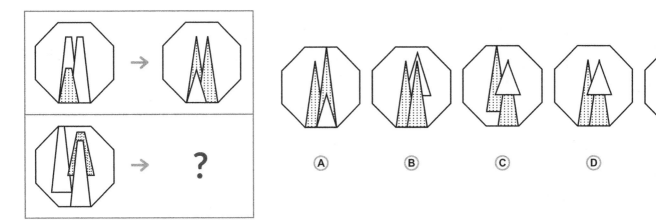

17

18

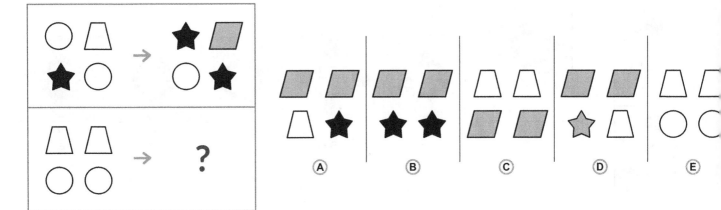

Paper Folding Directions: The top row shows a sheet of paper, how it was folded, and how holes were made in it. Which answer choice shows how the paper looks unfolded?

1

   Ⓐ   Ⓑ   Ⓒ   Ⓓ   Ⓔ

2

   Ⓐ   Ⓑ   Ⓒ   Ⓓ   Ⓔ

3

   Ⓐ   Ⓑ   Ⓒ   Ⓓ   Ⓔ

4

    Ⓐ   Ⓑ   Ⓒ   Ⓓ   Ⓔ

5

    Ⓐ   Ⓑ   Ⓒ   Ⓓ   Ⓔ

6

    Ⓐ   Ⓑ   Ⓒ   Ⓓ   Ⓔ

7

A   B   C   D   E

8

A   B   C   D   E

9

A   B   C   D   E

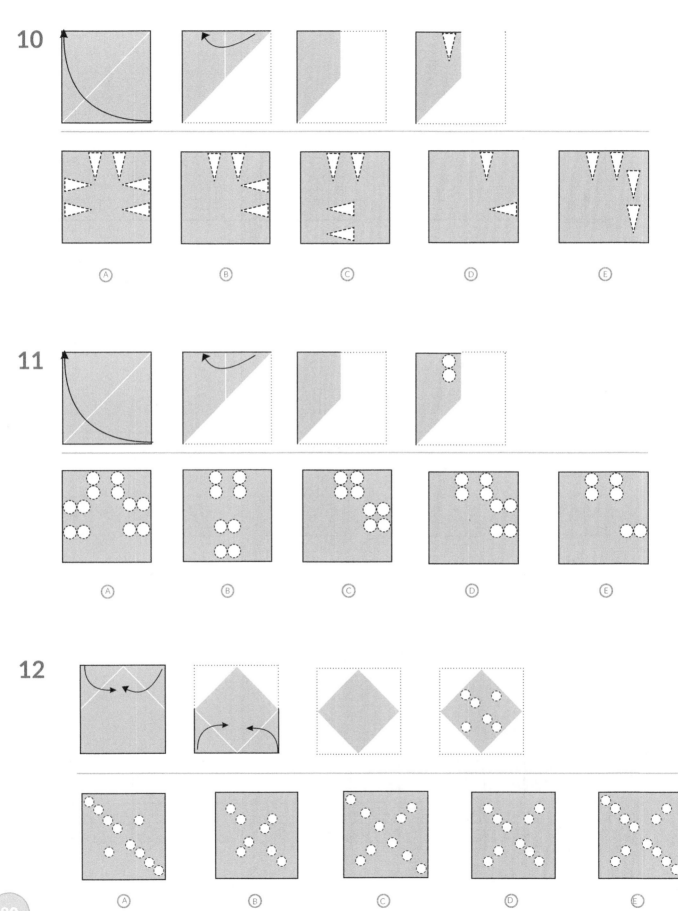

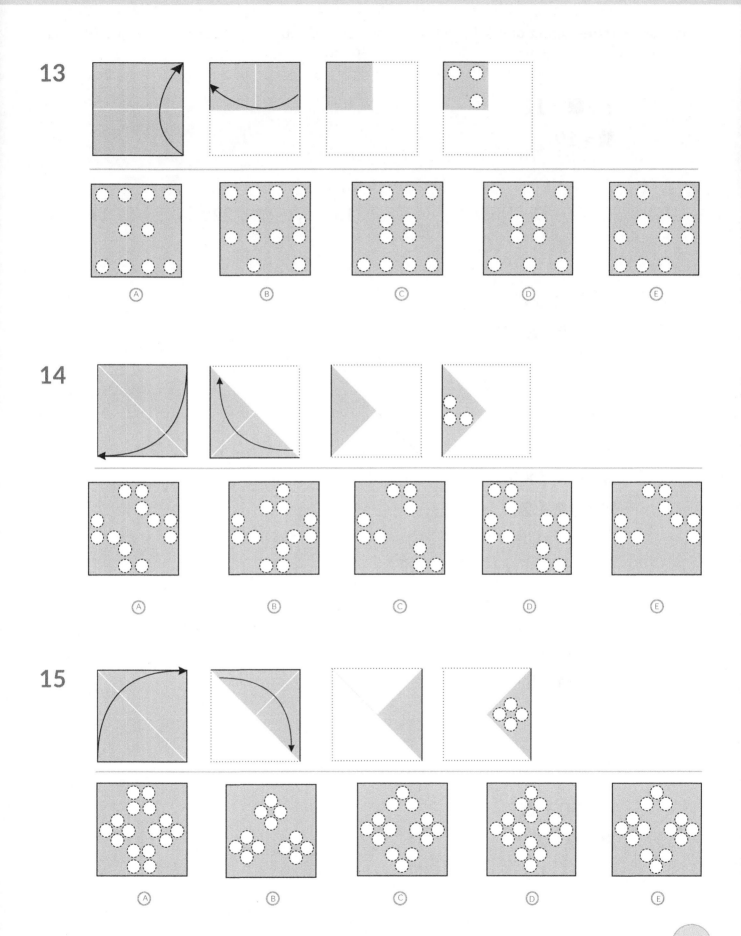

Number Puzzles Directions: What answer choice should you put in the place of the question mark so that both sides of the equal sign total the same amount?

1      $? \div \blacksquare = 12$

         $\blacksquare = 19$

    (A) 31   (B) 7   (C) 133   (D) 228   (E) 19

2      $? \times \blacksquare = 35$

         $13 - \blacksquare = 6$

    (A) 41   (B) 28   (C) 7   (D) 6   (E) 5

3      $\blacksquare - 4 = ? \times 2$

         $\blacksquare = 12 \div 2$

    (A) 4   (B) 2   (C) 1   (D) 6   (E) 3

4      $? - \blacksquare = 45$

         $20 - \blacksquare = 8 + 6$

    (A) 51   (B) 14   (C) 6   (D) 34   (E) 59

5      $? = 50 + \blacksquare$

         $\blacksquare = 9 \times 8$

    (A) 67   (B) 72   (C) 122   (D) 112   (E) 102

6 $3 + 2 \times (6-4) = 3 + ?$

    (A) 7   (B) 6   (C) 5   (D) 3   (E) 4

7 $? = \blacksquare + 7$

     $\bullet = \blacksquare \times 2$

     $\bullet = 10$

    (A) 10   (B) 11   (C) 15   (D) 12   (E) 13

8 $? - 5 = \blacksquare \div 6$

     $\blacksquare + 3 = 39$

    (A) 12   (B) 11   (C) 36   (D) 30   (E) 13

9 $? = \blacksquare + 7$

     $\bullet = \blacksquare \div 5$

     $\bullet = 2 \times 4$

    (A) 8   (B) 37   (C) 47   (D) 27   (E) 30

10 $? = \blacksquare + 9$

     $\bullet = \blacksquare \div 6$

     $\bullet = 21 \div 3$

    (A) 51   (B) 42   (C) 7   (D) 144   (E) 153

11

$? = \blacksquare + 12$

$\bullet = \blacksquare \div 9$

$\bullet = 4.0 \times 2.5$

   Ⓐ 10   Ⓑ 102   Ⓒ 112   Ⓓ 63   Ⓔ 75

12

$? - 6 = 5 \times \blacksquare$

$\blacksquare = 108 \div 18$

   Ⓐ 624   Ⓑ 6   Ⓒ 456   Ⓓ 56   Ⓔ 36

13

$? + 20 = 200 \div \blacksquare$

$\blacksquare + 50 = 70$

   Ⓐ 100   Ⓑ 200   Ⓒ -10   Ⓓ 20   Ⓔ 120

14

$? + 10 = 500 \div \blacksquare$

$\blacksquare + 60 = 80$

   Ⓐ 150   Ⓑ 140   Ⓒ 20   Ⓓ 15   Ⓔ 10

15

$? = \blacksquare + 15$

$\bullet = \blacksquare \times 7$

$\bullet = 7 \times 8$

   Ⓐ 23   Ⓑ 8   Ⓒ 56   Ⓓ 105   Ⓔ 15

16

$? = \blacksquare + 20$

$\bullet = \blacksquare \div 2$

$\bullet = 45.9 \div 5.1$

Ⓐ 40 Ⓑ 80 Ⓒ 100 Ⓓ 68 Ⓔ 38

17

$? = \blacksquare + 50$

$\bullet = \blacksquare \div 5$

$\bullet = 75.6 \div 2.52$

Ⓐ 30 Ⓑ 200 Ⓒ 100 Ⓓ 930 Ⓔ 980

18

$? = \blacksquare + 5$

$\bullet = \blacksquare \times 4$

$\bullet = 2.5 \times 3.2$

Ⓐ 7 Ⓑ 8 Ⓒ 9 Ⓓ 32 Ⓔ 13

19

$? = \blacksquare + 8$

$\bullet = \blacksquare \div 7$

$\bullet = \frac{3}{4} \times 12$

Ⓐ 9 Ⓑ 210 Ⓒ 281 Ⓓ 71 Ⓔ 63

20

$? = \blacksquare + 10$

$\bullet = \blacksquare \div 8$

$\bullet = 132 \div 12$

Ⓐ 11 Ⓑ 98 Ⓒ 960 Ⓓ 970 Ⓔ 1162

Number Analogies Directions: Look at the first two sets of numbers. Come up with a rule that both sets follow. Take this rule to figure out which answer choice goes in the place of the question mark.

1   [57 → 100]   [76 → 119]   [82 → ?]

      Ⓐ 43   Ⓑ 168   Ⓒ 116   Ⓓ 125   Ⓔ 44

2   [10 → 150]   [12 → 180]   [14 → ?]

      Ⓐ 215   Ⓑ 29   Ⓒ 196   Ⓓ 15   Ⓔ 210

3   [140 → 10]   [182 → 13]   [154 → ?]

      Ⓐ 11   Ⓑ 14   Ⓒ 12   Ⓓ 15   Ⓔ 10

4   [144 → 72]   [150 → 75]   [350 → ?]

      Ⓐ 150   Ⓑ 175   Ⓒ 125   Ⓓ 200   Ⓔ 225

5   [150 → 301]   [275 → 551]   [420 → ?]

      Ⓐ 840   Ⓑ 423   Ⓒ 841   Ⓓ 422   Ⓔ 842

6   [24 → 121]   [18 → 91]   [32 → ?]

      Ⓐ 37   Ⓑ 39   Ⓒ 159   Ⓓ 161   Ⓔ 150

7 [10 → 43]   [15 → 63]   [20 → ?]

Ⓐ 83   Ⓑ 77   Ⓒ 80   Ⓓ 26   Ⓔ 27

8 [75 → 17]   [90 → 20]   [65 → ?]

Ⓐ 13   Ⓑ 15   Ⓒ 11   Ⓓ 72   Ⓔ 70

9 [60 → 23]   [90 → 33]   [75 → ?]

Ⓐ 22   Ⓑ 20   Ⓒ 12   Ⓓ 25   Ⓔ 28

10 [12 → 144]   [14 → 196]   [15 → ?]

Ⓐ 30   Ⓑ 300   Ⓒ 150   Ⓓ 225   Ⓔ 240

11 [135 → 9]   [165 → 11]   [150 → ?]]

Ⓐ 10   Ⓑ 15   Ⓒ 20   Ⓓ 17   Ⓔ 13

12 [156 → 79]   [246 → 124]   [198 → ?]

Ⓐ 100   Ⓑ 99   Ⓒ 101   Ⓓ 98   Ⓔ 196

13 [486 → 27]   [360 → 20]   [252 → ?]

  (A) 13   (B) 14   (C) 15   (D) 12   (E) 18

14 [15/45 → 1/3]   [20/5 → 4]   [8/16 → ?]

  (A) 1/2   (B) 1/16   (C) 1/4   (D) 2   (E) 8

15 [200 → 102]   [150 → 77]   [180 → ?]

  (A) 90   (B) 92   (C) 94   (D) 88   (E) 80

16 [84 → 13]   [91 → 14]   [77 → ?]

  (A) 7   (B) 8   (C) 11   (D) 12   (E) 13

17 [72 → 11]   [90 → 13]   [81 → ?]

  (A) 9   (B) 6   (C) 12   (D) 15   (E) 80

18 [6 → 71]   [8 → 91]   [10 → ?]

  (A) 111   (B) 110   (C) 121   (D) 101   (E) 112

19   [80 → 14]   [64 → 12]   [88 → ?]

Ⓐ 11   Ⓑ 15   Ⓒ 7   Ⓓ 8   Ⓔ 16

20   [25 → 105]   [18 → 77]   [30 → ?]

Ⓐ 120   Ⓑ 115   Ⓒ 125   Ⓓ 39   Ⓔ 130

21   [36 → 114]   [40 → 126]   [42 → ?]

Ⓐ 126   Ⓑ 120   Ⓒ 130   Ⓓ 138   Ⓔ 132

22   [4→52]   [5→63]   [6→?]

Ⓐ 66   Ⓑ 11   Ⓒ 25   Ⓓ 58   Ⓔ 74

23   [99 → 15]   [108 → 16]   [117 → ?]

Ⓐ 9   Ⓑ 13   Ⓒ 18   Ⓓ 19   Ⓔ 17

Number Series Directions: Which answer choice would complete the pattern?

1
| 1   3   9   27   81   ? |

Ⓐ 162   Ⓑ 324   Ⓒ 243   Ⓓ 135   Ⓔ 130

2
123   180   237   294   351   ?

Ⓐ 408   Ⓑ 398   Ⓒ 357   Ⓓ 418   Ⓔ 428

3
15   14   12   11   9   ?

Ⓐ 5   Ⓑ 6   Ⓒ 7   Ⓓ 8   Ⓔ 3

4
5   16   28   41   55   ?

Ⓐ 70   Ⓑ 71   Ⓒ 69   Ⓓ 99   Ⓔ 72

5
62   63   64   66   67   68   70   71   ?

Ⓐ 70   Ⓑ 71   Ⓒ 72   Ⓓ 73   Ⓔ 74

6   3   12   6   24   12   48   ?

Ⓐ 3   Ⓑ 72   Ⓒ 12   Ⓓ 48   Ⓔ 24

7   9   18   19   38   39   ?

Ⓐ 40   Ⓑ 78   Ⓒ 79   Ⓓ 80   Ⓔ 41

8   12   15   10   17   20   15   22   25   ?

Ⓐ 20   Ⓑ 30   Ⓒ 32   Ⓓ 28   Ⓔ 31

9   60   48   61   49   62   50   63   51   ?

Ⓐ 52   Ⓑ 53   Ⓒ 65   Ⓓ 49   Ⓔ 64

10   85   60   84   61   83   62   82   63   ?

Ⓐ 80   Ⓑ 64   Ⓒ 81   Ⓓ 65   Ⓔ 82

11   4   6   8   7   9   11   10   12   ?

Ⓐ 13   Ⓑ 15   Ⓒ 10   Ⓓ 14   Ⓔ 16

12   3   4   5   4   6   8   6   9   12 ?

Ⓐ 9   Ⓑ 8   Ⓒ 7   Ⓓ 11   Ⓔ 10

13   2   6   18   6   18   54   18   54   162 ?

Ⓐ 18   Ⓑ 54   Ⓒ 81   Ⓓ 36   Ⓔ 126

14   121   116   124   118   113   121   115   110   118?

Ⓐ 110   Ⓑ 111   Ⓒ 113   Ⓓ 112   Ⓔ 126

15   89   80   72   65   59   54   50   47   ?

Ⓐ 45   Ⓑ 44   Ⓒ 43   Ⓓ 46   Ⓔ 48

16   51   -50   49   -48   47   -46 ?

Ⓐ 44   Ⓑ 45   Ⓒ -45   Ⓓ 46   Ⓔ -44

17   15   14   13   13   11   12   9   ?

Ⓐ 12   Ⓑ 10   Ⓒ 11   Ⓓ 9   Ⓔ 8

18　　**30　19　27　16　24　13 ?**

    Ⓐ 21　　　　Ⓑ 2　　　　Ⓒ 12　　　　Ⓓ 22　　　　Ⓔ 23

19　　**2　9　8　16　32　23　?**

    Ⓐ 30　　　　Ⓑ 92　　　　Ⓒ 120　　　　Ⓓ 64　　　　Ⓔ 128

20　　**15　9　14　10　13　11　?**

    Ⓐ 12　　　　Ⓑ 10　　　　Ⓒ 9　　　　Ⓓ 13　　　　Ⓔ 8

21　　**32　29　33　28　22　29　21　12　22　?**

    Ⓐ 21　　　　Ⓑ 11　　　　Ⓒ 43　　　　Ⓓ 13　　　　Ⓔ 10

22　　**3　6　24　48　192 ?**

    Ⓐ 292　　　　Ⓑ 288　　　　Ⓒ 384　　　　Ⓓ 374　　　　Ⓔ 394

23　　**50　47　51　46　40　47　39　30　40 ?**

    Ⓐ 19　　　　Ⓑ 22　　　　Ⓒ 50　　　　Ⓓ 31　　　　Ⓔ 29

- END OF PRACTICE TEST 2 -

PRACTICE TEST 1 ANSWER KEY

Verbal Classification, Practice Test 1

_____ 1. D. start, commence, kick off, and begin are all words meaning to initiate something or set something in motion by taking the first action

_____ 2. E. things that are usually green   _____ 3. A. how often something is done

_____ 4. C. baked foods   _____ 5. B. reptiles

_____ 6. C. jobs that involve fixing things -or- jobs involved in construction

_____ 7. A. vehicles with the primary purpose of transporting goods (vs. people)

_____ 8. B. words related to the position/orientation of a line or lines   _____ 9. C. living organisms

_____ 10. E. appliances used for heating things

_____ 11. D. verbs that have to do with increasing the amount of something _____ 12. D. parts of the digestive system

_____ 13. A. verbs that mean "to stop"   _____ 14. B. adjectives for a specific country

_____ 15. A. types of jobs that involve helping care for people   _____ 16. B. foods that come from animals

_____ 17. C. words that describe height   _____ 18. D. different kinds of bags

_____ 19. C. emotions that are feelings

_____ 20. A. words that have to do with coming together for a common purpose or goal

Questions Answered Correctly: _____ out of 20

Verbal Analogies, Practice Test 1

_____ 1. D. A florist works with flowers (to produce a finished product, a bouquet/flower arrangement). A sculptor works with clay (to produce a finished product, a sculpture).

_____ 2. C. Object > Purpose. The purpose of a life jacket is to float. The purpose of a seat belt is to restrain. (A seat belt does lock and it does fasten, but those are not its purpose.)

_____ 3. A. Object > Feeling; Silk feels smooth. Stone feels hard.

_____ 4. D. Building > Purpose; People go to a temple to worship. People go to a theatre to watch (a movie/play/concert).

_____ 5. B. An engineer is a type of profession. A fortress is a type of structure.

_____ 6. E. A symphony is created by a composer. A blueprint is created by an architect.

_____ 7. A. Scorching is a greater degree of being/feeling "hot", as ecstatic is a greater degree of being/feeling "happy".

_____ 8. C. (Greater degree) Something very loud is thunderous. Something very destructive is devastating.

_____ 9. D. A note is a small part of a melody. A step is a small part of a trek.

_____ 10. D. A teacher educates. A scientist researches.

_____ 11. C. If there is peace, there is no war. If there is silence, there is no noise.

_____ 12. D. Milk is produced by a cow, just as sap is produced by a tree.

_____ 13. C. Cacti are found in a desert just as bison are found on a prairie.

_____ 14. A. An adjective to describe lava is molten. An adjective to describe perfume is fragrant.

_____ 15. E. A flashlight is used to illuminate small, nearby areas, while a lighthouse is used to illuminate over long distances. A paintbrush is used for precise and detailed painting, while a paint roller is used for covering larger areas.

_____ 16. A. A shard is a small broken piece of glass. A splinter is a small, broken piece of wood.

_____ 17. E. opposites   _____ 18. A. synonyms   _____ 19. B. Darkness is a lack of light; chaos is a lack of order.

_____ 20. D. If something is still, there is no movement. If something is impeccable, it has no fault(s).

_____ 21. E. If you are skilled, you have acquired expertise. If you are educated, you have acquired knowledge.

_____ 22. E. Opposites

Questions Answered Correctly: _____ out of 22

Sentence Completion, Practice Test 1

_____ 1. B. asset = an advantage/a benefit   _____ 2. A. preference = to have more of a liking for one thing over others

_____ 3. E. fragile = easily broken   _____ 4. D. advance = move forward

_____ 5. A. arid = very dry   _____ 6. B. unique = one of a kind and different

_____ 7. C. apprehension = fear or anxiety that something bad will occur

_____ 8. B. significantly = something happening in a big or important way

_____ 9. E. agitated = to feel nervous or upset, and often restless   _____ 10. B. revenue = income; money coming in

_____ 11. D. assess = to evaluate/analyze; foundation = the principle of something/the basis of something

_____ 12. E. intensify = to become more intense/to become stronger; promptly = without delay

_____ 13. A. unpredictable = likely to change suddenly, not able to be predicted; urge = to strongly encourage someone/to strongly advise someone to do something

_____ 14. B. jubilant = feeling lots of joy; invigorated = to be filled with energy

_____ 15. D. ensure = to make sure; distinct = clearly different from others of a similar kind

_____ 16. A. unexpected = not expected; complex = not simple

_____ 17. E. maintain = to enable something to continue; essential = necessary/very important

_____ 18. A. congregate = to gather; occasion = a special time/an important time for an event

_____ 19. C. common = found often; originate = to come from originally

_____ 20. B. bias = favoring one side vs. the other, in a way that is not fair; appealed = made a request to a higher authority to review and change a decision

Questions Answered Correctly: _____ out of 20

Figure Classification, Practice Test 1

_____ 1. E. triangles pointing left
_____ 2. E. a heart & trapezoid are inside the square's sections & they are opposite each other
_____ 3. A. 8-sided shapes
_____ 4. D. shapes alternate: gray, then dotted
_____ 5. B. inside shape is 1 circle of each color: black, white, gray
_____ 6. C. 1 of each shape: down-pointing pentagon, diamond, star -and- 1 is either gray, dotted, or black
_____ 7. E. right shape has 1 more side than left shape
_____ 8. D. half of shape is black/half is dotted
_____ 9. D. the bottom shape is the same as the top shape, but has been rotated 90° clockwise (to the right)
_____ 10. A. as figures rotate, octagon remains at same point on "L" shape -OR- figures rotate 90° counterclockwise
_____ 11. B. small center shape & outer shape have same design (or color) inside -and- the shapes are different kinds of shapes
_____ 12. E. 1 shape points up, 3 shapes point down
_____ 13. D. in the group of 2 shapes, the larger shape has 1 more side than the smaller shape
_____ 14. D. Inside square are 3 shapes: octagon that's next to rectangle and a diamond that is not
_____ 15. A. tic-tac-toe with ovals
_____ 16. C. diagonal line goes from upper left to lower right inside shape
_____ 17. B. one-quarter of shape has been "cut"
_____ 18. B. order of shapes: diamond - crescent - octagon
_____ 19. C. the square is divided into 3 triangles; in the largest is a pentagon; in the smaller 2 & on opposite sides as the pentagon is a rectangle & half-circle

Questions Answered Correctly: _____ out of 19

Figure Analogies, Practice Test 1

_____ 1. B.
_____ 2. A. outer shape gets smaller and moves to center of the cluster of lines (on top, it's a hexagon; on bottom, it's an octagon) -and- the smaller shape is white/you can't see the line cluster behind the white shape
_____ 3. D. colors switch in the divided square; colors switch in the divided hexagon
_____ 4. A. larger outer top shape moves to the bottom
_____ 5. E. shapes "flip" to become a mirror image
_____ 6. D. gray rectangle flips to cover the left side of the middle shape and the 2 colored squares are under the middle shape
_____ 7. A. shape group rotates 90° counterclockwise & the outer 2 smaller shapes change color
_____ 8. C. since the figures are the same, they change the same way
_____ 9. E. dark gray becomes light gray; white becomes dark gray; light gray becomes white -or- the last shape becomes the first shape
_____ 10. D: group of triangles "flips"/is a mirror image (note that in the bottom box, when you flip the 2 shapes on the right, choice D is the only choice with the dark gray arrow & white shapes flipped correctly)
_____ 11. B. top shape goes inside bottom shape & gets bigger; middle shape goes inside & rotates 90° clockwise
_____ 12. D: left arrrow=square; down arrow=triangle pointing up; up arrow = heart;
_____ 13. A. from left to right, larger shape will have 2 less sides, smaller shape will have +1 side; colors of large & small shapes reverse
_____ 14. D. top shape rotates 180°; shape on left moves to right; bottom shape flips & changes from light gray to dark gray
_____ 15. E: shapes change to hexagons; note that the shapes are divided into quarters & the dark quarters change positions change like this (bottom left > bottom right; top left > bottom left; bottom right > top left; top right > top right)
_____ 16. B. upper left figure rotates 180° to face down; Upper right & lower right shapes switch and the new upper right becomes gray
_____ 17. C. the bottom moves to the top; the top moves to the middle; the middle goes to the bottom. Then the shapes are placed over each other rather than under
_____ 18. C. top shape goes inside middle shape; top shape & middle shape get bigger; bottom shape becomes the center shape, rotates 90° counterclockwise, and turns gray
_____ 19. A. shape group rotates 180°

Questions Answered Correctly: _____ out of 19

Paper Folding, Practice Test 1

_____ 1. D	_____ 2. E	_____ 3. B	_____ 4. C	_____ 5. D	_____ 6. A	_____ 7. C
_____ 8. C	_____ 9. D	_____ 10. E	_____ 11. A	_____ 12. E	_____ 13. D	_____ 14. C
_____ 15. E	_____ 16. B	_____ 17. A				

Questions Answered Correctly: _____ out of 17

Number Puzzles, Practice Test 1

_____ 1. C	_____ 2. B	_____ 3. E	_____ 4. C	_____ 5. A	_____ 6. B	_____ 7. A	_____ 8. D
_____ 9. C	_____ 10. D	_____ 11. B	_____ 12. E	_____ 13. D	_____ 14. B	_____ 15. A	_____ 16. A
_____ 17. E							

Questions Answered Correctly: _____ out of 17

Number Analogies, Practice Test 1

_____ 1. D. -19 _____ 2. E. +28 _____ 3. A. x8 _____ 4. B. half _____ 5. C. squared
_____ 6. A. ÷10 _____ 7. B. ÷10 _____ 8. E. reduced _____ 9. E. x13 _____ 10. D. x2, then +1
_____ 11. B. x2, then -1 _____ 12. C. ÷2, then +1 _____ 13. A. x3, then +2 _____ 14. D. ×4 , then +1
_____ 15. E. squared _____ 16. B. ÷9 _____ 17. D. x4 _____ 18. E. ÷4, then +1 _____ 19. A. -8
_____ 20. E. ÷3, then +1 _____ 21. E. x 4, then add 1 _____ 22. C. ÷5, then +1 _____ 23. B. x3, then +4

Questions Answered Correctly: _____ out of 23

Number Series, Practice Test 1

_____ 1.D. x2 _____ 2. B. +22 _____ 3. C. -38
_____ 4. A. begins w/47, every other number is 47; then, starting with 53, every other number is +5
_____ 5. E. -1, -2, -1, -2, etc. _____ 6. A. -11, -12, -13, -14, -15, etc.
_____ 7. D. +1, +1, +2; +1, +1, +2 _____ 8. E. x2, +1, x2, +1, etc. _____ 9. B. X4, ÷2, X4, ÷2, etc.
_____ 10. D. +3, -5, +7, +3, -5, +7, etc.
_____ 11. D. the numbers in spaces 1, 3, 5, 7, 9 increase by 1; the numbers in spaces 2, 4, 6, 8 increase by 1 -OR the difference in each pair of numbers is 11 (50 & 39; 51 & 40, etc.)
_____ 12. C. the numbers in spaces 1, 3, 5, 7, 9 decrease by 1; the numbers in spaces 2, 4, 6, 8 increase by 1
_____ 13. E. +2, +2, -1, +2, +2, -1, etc. _____ 14. A. +1, +1, -1; +2, +2, -2; +3, +3, -3
_____ 15. C. ×2, ×2, ÷2, ×2, ×2, ÷2, etc. _____ 16. B. -5, +8, -6, -5, +8, -6 _____ 17. A. +3, +4, +5, +6, +7, +8, +9
_____ 18. C. digits decrease by 1 -AND- the signs alternate between positive and negative
_____ 19. E. starting with 12, the number decreases by 2 every other number -and- starting with 11, the number decreases by 1
_____ 20. D. every other number, starting with 5, is 3 times the previous -and- every other number, starting w/13, increases by 9
_____ 21. C. -6, +5, -4, +3, -2, +1 OR every other number starting with 10 decreases by 1 -and- starting with 4, increases by 1
_____ 22. B. ×2, ×3, ×2, ×3, etc.
_____ 23. A. -3, +4, -5 | -6, +7, -8 | -9 ,+10, -11

Questions Answered Correctly: _____ out of 23

PRACTICE TEST 2 ANSWER KEY

Verbal Classification, Practice Test 2

_____ 1. E. parts of the skeletal system _____ 2. B. words having to do with how see-through an object is
_____ 3. C. shades of red _____ 4. D. objects in which you put things
_____ 5. B. foods that must be cooked to eat _____ 6. C. adjectives that describe something in a very limited amount
_____ 7. A. words having to do with colleges/universities _____ 8. D. different types of fabric
_____ 9. B. words having to do with the bottom or the lowest point of something
_____ 10. A. different genres of books _____ 11. E. liquids _____ 12. B. things that have screens
_____ 13. B. transportation that carries many people at once _____ 14. D. units of time
_____ 15. C. machines that dispense things (an ATM dispenses cash, vending machines dispense snacks, a soda fountain dispenses soda, a fuel pump dispenses fuel)
_____ 16. C. words having to do with an increase _____ 17. A. empires in history
_____ 18. B. words meaning to form an idea of the value or amount of something
_____ 19. E. words that have to do with enemies

Questions Answered Correctly: _____ out of 19

Verbal Analogies, Practice Test 2

_____ 1. D. Enormous means very large. Freezing means very cold.
_____ 2. A. Something heavy is defined by its great weight, like something fast is defined by its high speed.
_____ 3. B. A theater is a place where movies are shown, like a museum is a place where artifacts are displayed/shown.
_____ 4. E. Opposites _____ 5. A. A spark might cause a fire, like a flood might cause a landslide.
_____ 6. C. A wagon was used in the past for transportation, like a car is used today, and a typewriter was used in the past for typing documents, like a computer is used today.
_____ 7. E. The top of a building is the roof. The top of a forest is the canopy.
_____ 8. D. A firework explodes and something is released (light). A balloon bursts and something is released (air).
_____ 9. C. Pollution harms the environment. Dishonesty harms trust. _____ 10. E. Synonyms
_____ 11. D. A lung fills with air. Without air, the lung cannot serve its main function — breathing. An engine fills with fuel. Without fuel, the engine cannot serve its main function — powering the vehicle.
_____ 12. A. Something very exciting is thrilling. Something very noteworthy is remarkable.
_____ 13. B. Opposites _____ 14. B. Neglect is a lack of care, like ignorance is a lack of knowledge.
_____ 15. E. A storm might cause a flood, like a drought might cause a famine.
_____ 16. B. A flashlight is a modern tool for providing light, replacing the older lantern, just as a clock is a modern tool for telling time, replacing the older sundial.
_____ 17. C. Something that is cryptic is something hard to decipher. An obstacle is something hard to overcome.
_____ 18. A. When the vibrancy of something decreases, it fades. When the size of something decreases, it contracts.
_____ 19. C. Antonyms _____ 20. A. Synonyms
_____ 21. B. When someone is innocent, they are without guilt. When someone/something is aimless, they are without direction.
_____ 22. D. Hierarchical means organized according to rank. Something that is geographical is organized according to location.

Questions Answered Correctly: _____ out of 22

Sentence Completion, Practice Test 2

_____ 1. B. obtain = to get   _____ 2. C. optimal = best
_____ 3. A. contrasting = differing in very obvious/striking ways   _____ 4. E. enhance = to raise, to make more intense
_____ 5. D. irrelevant = not relevant/not significant or important _____ 6. A. rancid = strong smelling in a bad way; rotten
_____ 7. C. proficient = advanced/competent/an expert in a certain area
_____ 8. B. ally = here, an ally is a person that provides help and support
_____ 9. A. cultivate = to develop or improve with training   _____ 10. B. rage = very fierce anger
_____ 11. E. trepidation = a combination of fear and dread about something that might happen
_____ 12. B. scarcely = hardly/barely; harsh = very uncomfortable/unpleasant/stark
_____ 13. D. anticipate = to expect/to be sure of; chaotic = full of chaos/completely confusing
_____ 14. E. provides = to supply something that is needed; subsequent = coming after or later
_____ 15. C. abundant = well supplied, in great quantity; powerful = strong/having great power
_____ 16. E. strenuous = demanding, requiring lots of effort; depths = distance from the surface (of the water)
_____ 17. D. distinct = different from other similar things; exceptional = outstanding
_____ 18. B. entrench = set so firmly that it's unlikely to change; dislodge = to force out or to force to move
_____ 19. A. mitigate = to lessen the bad effects of something; implement = to put into effect

Questions Answered Correctly: _____ out of 19

Figure Classification, Practice Test 2

_____ 1. E. inside larger shape are 2 small vertically-aligned octagons with same color
_____ 2. B. inside circle is a: star, circle, square, heart   _____ 3. A. 6-sided shape with a smaller 6-sided shape inside
_____ 4. B. in circle are 3 shapes, 2 are the same kind of shape & same size; 1 is black & 1 is white; a 3rd shape is white
_____ 5. D. diamond is divided into equal parts   _____ 6. A. dotted shape has 1 more side than white shape
_____ 7. C. as triangle rotates, its sections remain in the same order and the triangle must be the same size (D is smaller)
_____ 8. E. each group has a circle, parallelogram, pentagon; they are either gray or white
_____ 9. C. square has straight lines that are aligned vertically
_____ 10. A. 1 darker gray & 1 lighter gray opposite each other; 4 sections of circle have different designs
_____ 11. A. 3 triangles & 6 circles (the top 3 figures also each have 2 dark gray circles; however, more than 1 answer choice has 2 dark gray circles, so this can't be the answer)
_____ 12. D. larger shape has diagonal lines going from upper left to lower right
_____ 13. E. squares have formed "tic-tac-toe", plus a single diamond is in a corner
_____ 14. B. when you put the shape group on its base (the double lines) the order is the same
_____ 15. E. 1 corner (and only 1 corner) has the same group of 3 shapes: parallelogram on top, oval & diamond on bottom
_____ 16. C. star & heart are in opposite sections of the divided larger shape (star & heart must be opposite each other)
_____ 17. A. the bottom shape is the same as the top shape, but it has been rotated 90° clockwise (to the right)
_____ 18. D. larger shapes & smaller triangles are different colors -and- the triangles point to one of the larger shape's corners

Questions Answered Correctly: _____ out of 18

Figure Analogies, Practice Test 2

_____ 1. E. gray shape 'flips' down, dotted shape added on top that's facing the original position of the first shape
_____ 2. D. in the sections of the squares/parallelograms, the colors/designs change like this: dotted becomes black, black becomes white, and white becomes dotted; also, the original outer shape does not change
_____ 3. A. bottom shape becomes top shape & gets smaller, middle shape becomes bottom shape & gets bigger, top shape becomes middle shape & gets bigger
_____ 4. B. the shape group rotates 90° clockwise, then the gray circles become white and vice versa
_____ 5. C. on top, dark gray rectangle with 1/4 filled w/ light gray becomes a circle filled with dots and the same amount (1/4) filled with light gray; on the bottom, the dotted rectangle with 1/2 filled w/ lighter gray becomes dark gray circle with same amount (1/2) filled with dark gray; note that the design & quantity of the inside lines must be the same also
_____ 6. A. group of figures shows 3 "half" shapes; from left to right, largest half has 5 sides, then 3 sides; middle half points down, then up; smallest half has rounded corners, then a version of this same half, but with straight corners
_____ 7. D. mirror image of original figure
_____ 8. C. division sign becomes "O"; minus becomes plus; "O" becomes division sign
_____ 9. C. in top set, square switches from gray to dotted; lower left parallelogram changes to a pentagon, moves to the upper right, and the design inside changes from dots to gray; in the bottom, the reverse occurs: square changes from dotted to gray, parallelogram changes to a pentagon & changes its position and design (gray to dotted); no change with rectangle
_____ 10. E. small shapes change from diamonds to squares and are horizontally aligned & all except 1 of changes from dotted to dark gray
_____ 11. B. corners of shape become rounded & middle line gets longer
_____ 12. E. shape rotates 180° & wavy lines become light gray
_____ 13. A. shape group becomes a "mirror image", then the hexagon moves in front of the diamond and turns white; diamond changes from dark gray to light gray; large square changes from light gray to dark gray
_____ 14. C. inside & outside shape switch positions & both get smaller; with the new inner shape (the octagon), the lined pattern & the solid color have switched; with the new outer shape (the diamond), the gray & the solid color remain the same
_____ 15. D. white triangles become black diamonds; center shape (the arch) rotates 180°; one more octagon is added -and- all the octagons change from black to gray
_____ 16. E. shapes in first box (thin trapezoids) change to triangles & the colors/patterns of the shapes reverse
_____ 17. B. order of shapes reverses -and- the 2nd shape & the 4th shape turn gray
_____ 18. B. white circles become black stars; white trapezoids become gray parallelograms; black stars become white circles

Questions Answered Correctly: _____ out of 18

Paper Folding, Practice Test 2

_____ 1. B _____ 2. B _____ 3. D _____ 4. C _____ 5. A _____ 6. E _____ 7. C
_____ 8. D _____ 9. C _____ 10. B _____ 11. D _____ 12. E _____ 13. C _____ 14. A
_____ 15. D

Questions Answered Correctly: _____ out of 15

Number Puzzles, Practice Test 2

_____ 1. D _____ 2. E _____ 3. C _____ 4. A _____ 5. C _____ 6. E _____ 7. D _____ 8. B
_____ 9. C _____ 10. A _____ 11. B _____ 12. E _____ 13. C _____ 14. D _____ 15. A _____ 16. E
_____ 17. B _____ 18. A _____ 19. D _____ 20. B

Questions Answered Correctly: _____ out of 20

Number Analogies, Practice Test 2

_____ 1. D. +43 _____ 2. E. x15 _____ 3. A. ÷14 _____ 4. B. half _____ 5. C. x2, then +1
_____ 6. D. x5, then +1 _____ 7. A. x4, then +3 _____ 8. B. ÷5, then +2 _____ 9. E. ÷3, then +3 _____ 10. D. squared
_____ 11. A. ÷15 _____ 12. A. ÷2, then +1 _____ 13. B. ÷18 _____ 14. A. reduced
_____ 15. B. ÷2, then +2 _____ 16. D. ÷7, then +1 _____ 17. C. ÷9, then +3
_____ 18. A. x10, then +11 _____ 19. B. ÷8, then +4 _____ 20. C. x4, then +5 _____ 21. E. x3, then +6
_____ 22. E. x11, then +8 _____ 23. E. ÷9, then add 4

Questions Answered Correctly: _____ out of 23

Number Series, Practice Test 2

_____ 1. C. x3 _____ 2. A. +57 _____ 3. D. -1, -2, -1, -2, etc.
_____ 4. A. +11, +12, +13, +14, +15, etc. _____ 5. C. +1, +1, +2; +1, +1, +2 _____ 6. E. X4, ÷2, X4, ÷2, etc.
_____ 7. B. x2, +1, x2, +1, etc. _____ 8. A. +3, -5, +7, +3, -5, +7, etc.
_____ 9. E. the numbers in spaces 1, 3, 5, 7, 9 increase by 1; the numbers in spaces 2, 4, 6, 8 increase by 1 -OR the difference in each pair of numbers is 12
_____ 10. C. the numbers in spaces 1, 3, 5, 7, 9 decrease by 1; the numbers in spaces 2, 4, 6, 8 increase by 1
_____ 11. D. +2, +2, -1, +2, +2, -1, etc. _____ 12. A. +1, +1, -1; +2, +2, -2; +3, +3, -3
_____ 13. B. ×3, ×3, ÷3, ×3, ×3, ÷3, etc. _____ 14. D. -5, +8, -6, -5, +8, -6
_____ 15. A. -9, -8, -7, -6, -5, -4 _____ 16. B. signs alternate positive & negative; the digits decrease by 1
_____ 17. C. starting with 15, the number decreases by 2 every other number -and- starting with 14, the number decreases by 1 every other number
_____ 18. A. -11, +8, -11, +8
_____ 19. E. every other number, starting with 2, is 4 times the previous number -and- every other number, starting with 9, increases by 7
_____ 20. A. -6, +5, -4, +3, -2, +1 _____ 21. B. -3, +4, -5 | -6, +7, -8 | -9 ,+10, -11
_____ 22. C. ×2, ×4, ×2, ×4, etc.
_____ 23. E. -3, +4, -5 | -6, +7, -8 | -9 ,+10, -11

Questions Answered Correctly: _____ out of 23

Check out our other books for
COGAT® K to Grade 5

www.GatewayGifted.com

Made in the USA
Las Vegas, NV
25 October 2024

10456087R00057